EATING WITH
UNCLE SAM

RECIPES AND HISTORICAL BITES FROM THE
NATIONAL ARCHIVES

WITH A MESSAGE FROM DAVID S. FERRIERO, ARCHIVIST OF THE UNITED STATES

INTRODUCTION BY CHEF JOSÉ ANDRÉS

EDITED BY PATTY REINERT MASON

THE FOUNDATION FOR THE NATIONAL ARCHIVES, WASHINGTON, DC

IN ASSOCIATION WITH D GILES LIMITED, LONDON

Eating with Uncle Sam
Recipes and Historical Bites from the National Archives

Edited by Patty Reinert Mason
Designed by Brian Barth
Copyedited by Maureen MacDonald

First published in 2011 by GILES
an imprint of D Giles Limited
4 Crescent Stables, 139 Upper Richmond Road
London, SW15 2TN, UK
www.gilesltd.com

Library of Congress Control Number: 2011928986

ISBN: 978-1-907804-00-7

FOUNDATION FOR THE
NATIONAL
ARCHIVES

Foundation for the National Archives
Thora Colot, Executive Director
Patty Reinert Mason, Director of Publications
Kathleen Lietzau, Publications and Research
Assistant

**National Archives and Records
Administration**
Brian Barth, Designer
Maureen MacDonald, Copyeditor

GILES
David Rose, Proofreader

Produced by the Publisher, an imprint of
D Giles Limited
Printed and bound in Canada

Photographic Credits
The majority of images reproduced in this book
are from the holdings of the National Archives,
which, unless otherwise noted, supplied the
photographs.

Front cover and opposite: Know Your Onions poster,
ca. 1943, adapted. See page 41.

Editor's Note
The recipes in *Eating with Uncle Sam: Recipes
and Historical Bites from the National Archives*
were selected from thousands of recipes in the
holdings of the National Archives, including
its 13 Presidential libraries and museums. The
book includes recipes from World Wars I and
II, when Americans, considering it patriotic
to conserve food in support of troops fighting
overseas, consulted such Government recipe
pamphlets as *Potato Possibilities, Sweets without
Sugar,* and *Without Wheat.*

Also included are recipes from the wildly
popular *Aunt Sammy's Radio Recipes,* published
by the U.S. Department of Agriculture to
fulfill requests for recipes that the character
"Aunt Sammy," the "wife" of the mythical
"Uncle Sam," had shared with radio listeners
nationwide since 1926. Still other recipes come
from the records of the Depression-era Work
Projects Administration's Federal Writers'
Project, which sent writers around the country
to write about the food and culture of America,
and from the culinary records of the U.S.
military and the Federal school lunch program.
Finally, the book includes often-requested dishes
from the recipe boxes of U.S. Presidents.

In an effort to keep the language of the
recipes true to their eras and sources, the
recipes are published as originally written.
If the Queen of England measures with
a "teacup," who are we to change this to
a lowly "cup"? If President Eisenhower
recommends, "good celery," a "good-sized
onion," or "nice-sized carrots," we assume
his meaning is clear to those who knew his
tastes or open to the cook's interpretation.
The same goes for Aunt Sammy's or school
lunch recipes that list an ingredient simply
as "fat." No attempt has been made to test,
update, or modify the recipes to render them
healthier by today's standards. This is, after
all, a historical recipe book.

TABLE OF CONTENTS

Message from the Archivist iv

Introduction by José Andrés vi

MESSAGE FROM THE ARCHIVIST OF THE UNITED STATES

David S. Ferriero

Windows on the World Restaurant on the 107th floor of the World Trade Center was always a destination for special celebrations. Sitting high above the city, eye level with passing planes, one had an extraordinary view of the Manhattan skyline.

One of my favorite desserts was called "Windows on the World White Chocolate Mousse." I ordered it on several occasions, enjoying the "cloud of white chocolate floating on the dark chocolate base." I loved the way the chocolate layers, when sliced, made a perfect little sailboat of mousse. I finally wrote to the restaurant to ask for the recipe.

My first attempt turned the floating cloud to cement, sinking my boat! But I later discovered that by adding more water to the gelatin, I could recreate this delectable sensation in my own kitchen. It has since become a specialty I serve to family and friends in my new home in Washington, DC.

Today, every time I read this recipe, it brings to mind the sadness of the September 11 terrorist attacks. While I remember all those who worked at this elegant restaurant and in the World Trade Center who were lost on that historic day, I am also thankful for the memories of what once was.

This recipe, like all great recipes, evokes wonderful memories of special times and of the people with whom we have dined.

The recipes in *Eating with Uncle Sam: Recipes and Historical Bites from the National Archives* were culled from thousands of recipes that have made their way into the vast holdings of the National Archives. Some—"Portuguese Blood Pudding" from Martha's Vineyard and "Jambalaya à la Créole" from New Orleans, for example—were discovered in the records of the Work Projects Administration, which sent Depression-era writers around the country to document the food and culture of America's diverse population. Some, like "Scalloped Onions and Peanuts," come from the Department of Agriculture's "Aunt Sammy's" radio shows from the 1920s, which created a fictitious wife for the mythical "Uncle Sam" who shared homemaking advice and her economical and nutritious recipes with housewives around the nation. Still others come from the cookbooks of the military and from Federal school lunch programs, which taught Americans how to save food resources during wartime and influenced our still-evolving understanding of what constitutes a nutritious meal for growing children.

Many more—including "Laura Bush's Guacamole" and "JFK's Favorite Fish Chowder"—come from our 13 Presidential libraries and museums. They show how our leaders from many regions of the country brought their eating habits and cuisine to the White House and popularized certain dishes as everyday Americans wrote to Presidents and First Ladies to request their favorite recipes.

I hope these recipes will not only inspire you to create your own food memories but will also give you a taste of the incredible diversity of records held in trust for the American people by the National Archives.

WINDOWS ON THE WORLD WHITE CHOCOLATE MOUSSE

WHITE CHOCOLATE LAYER:

12 ounces white chocolate bits

3 cups heavy cream

4 egg yolks

¾ cup sugar

2 envelopes (2 tablespoons) unflavored gelatin

½ cup warm water

Melt chocolate in a double boiler over simmering water. Cool. Meanwhile, whip cream until stiff and refrigerate until needed. Beat egg yolks and sugar together until pale and triple in volume. Soften gelatin in warm water; heat slightly to dissolve. Cool slightly. Add a scoop of beaten yolks to gelatin and mix well. Add gelatin mixture to remaining yolks, beating constantly. Add melted chocolate, one third at a time, beating at low speed. Mix in whipped cream, stirring constantly. Pour mixture into 8-cup dome-shaped mold. Refrigerate 1½ hours.

DARK CHOCOLATE LAYER:

24 ounces dark semi-sweet chocolate bits

1½ cups heavy cream

6 tablespoons sugar

3 tablespoons butter

1½ tablespoons Grand Marnier

Bring butter, sugar, and cream just to the boil. Add chocolate bits, remove from heat, and stir until the chocolate has melted. Cool at room temperature for one hour. Then refrigerate until hard—a couple of hours. When ready to use, beat it with the Grand Marnier until it has softened.

Add the dark chocolate layer to the white chocolate layer and spread evenly. Refrigerate until set. When ready to serve place the mold in warm water for 5–10 seconds and invert onto serving platter. An elegant cloud of white chocolate floats on the dark chocolate base.

Background: World Trade Center in New York City, 1974. *Records of the Environmental Protection Agency.*

INTRODUCTION

José Andrés

American cooking is something I find so fascinating. When the National Archives came to me with their "What's Cooking, Uncle Sam?" exhibition project, I had to be part of it. For me, cooking is better than any history or guidebook. It tells you everything about a country, about a people. We all eat, and food is the easiest point of entry to understand a culture. This cookbook *Eating with Uncle Sam* is a fascinating selection of the thousands of recipes and documents related to food that have made their way into the Archives' collection.

Few people realize that there was a large market, Center Market, on the current site of the National Archives. From about 1870 to 1930, Center Market offered Washingtonians a place to purchase fresh fruit and vegetables, meat, and eggs from all over the region. It drew everyone from Presidents and First Ladies to average working people. Farmers would make their way down Brookville Pike or from across the river in Virginia and bring their goods to market.

My love affair with America and its food has been a lifelong one. As a boy, growing up in Barcelona, dreaming of America, the place I envisioned was loud and colorful, optimistic and cheerful, a place almost like Oz. When I thought of the food I thought of what I saw in the films of Hollywood, of Charlie Chaplin eating a shoe in *The Gold Rush,* of all-night diners, of hamburgers, of Coca-Cola, of hot dog carts, of impossibly tall pastel-colored frosted layer cakes, of Bob Hope eating sole out of a woman's shoe at a surrealist dinner hosted by Salvador Dalí, of boxes of cereal, of fruit pies and doughnuts, of cattle drives, of acres and acres of wheat under a Midwestern sky, of abundance.

Then I came to America as a young adult and, like many Europeans, I had to let go of those notions. The gastronomic tradition I found here was much richer, much more profound than I expected. In fact, today I spend a lot of time explaining to the rest of the world that Americans don't survive on a diet of hamburgers alone and that American food is actually more complex and layered than they might expect. The idea of a melting pot is never more true than at the American table where the heritage of the many peoples who have lived here and have found their way here have combined to create a unique national cuisine.

The first place I ever visited in the United States was Pensacola, Florida, as a young sailor in the Spanish navy. This city that has been under so many flags, the Spanish, the British, the French, the Confederates, the American, was a perfect place to begin my exploration of American food. Everything was on the plate: who these people were, where they came from, what the land was like, what fish and seafood the local waters produced.

Like many of the people in Pensacola, my roots lie somewhere else. My story is a very American story, a classic immigrant story. I came here from Spain and one of the ways I stay connected to home is to cook the food I grew up with. This is something that millions of people have done before me, the waves of different peoples from different cultures who brought their food traditions to America and sought to preserve them. So often, these dishes soon find their way into the American menu, like sauerkraut, curry, and even the gazpacho of my home, all recipes found in these pages.

Americans are very universal in their tastes, much more so than Europeans. Compared to a European, Americans consume a staggering variety of cuisines and foods in an average week. If it is good, no matter where it comes from, Americans will adopt it, adapt it, and make it their own.

Technologies like refrigeration and railroads further opened up possibilities for Americans. Now Americans were no longer limited to what grew in their backyard or what was in season. Food could be preserved and brought from farther away: strawberries from California, lobsters from Maine, peaches from Georgia.

What we eat today isn't just about immigration or the land or technology, it is also about the hand of Government, both directly and indirectly influencing what we eat. The necessities of wartime brought publications like *Without Wheat, Sweets without Sugar,* and *Potato Possibilities.* Recipes that used grains other than wheat, like Oatmeal Peanut Biscuits or Barley-Rye Biscuits or conserves made without sugar like Plum Conserve, sought to discourage civilian consumption of commodities needed for the war effort. Whether on the farm, in the factory, in the kitchen, or at the table, the Government has affected food choices and influenced how we think about feeding ourselves.

This neighborhood has always been a hub for food, and just steps away from the National Archives, we've opened America Eats, a restaurant devoted to over 200 years of American cooking. Named for the Work Projects Administration's Federal Writers' Project of the 1930s, this restaurant was inspired by the same rich history of American food found in the National Archives Experience exhibition "What's Cooking, Uncle Sam?" and this recipe book *Eating with Uncle Sam.* I hope you will visit and continue to explore our fascinating shared story on a plate.

Background: A fruit and vegetable stand in Center Market, Washington, DC, which was later replaced by the National Archives Building, 1915. *Records of the Bureau of Agricultural Economics.*

Dear Mr. President,

Seeing a picture of you in today's newspaper standing in front of a barbecue grilling quail, reminded me that I had never sent you the recipe of the drop scones which I promised you at Balmoral. I now hasten to do so, and I do hope you will find them successful.

Though the quantities are for 16 people, when there are fewer, I generally put in less flour and milk, but use the other ingredients as stated.

I have also tried using golden syrup or Treacle instead of only sugar and that can be very good, too.

I think the mixture needs a great deal of beating while making, and shouldn't stand about too long before cooking …

Yours sincerely,
Elizabeth R

Letter from Queen Elizabeth II to President Dwight D. Eisenhower, January 24, 1960. *Opposite:* President Dwight D. Eisenhower and Queen Elizabeth II in Montreal, Canada, June 26, 1959. *Inset:* First page of the Queen's letter. *Dwight D. Eisenhower Presidential Library and Museum.*

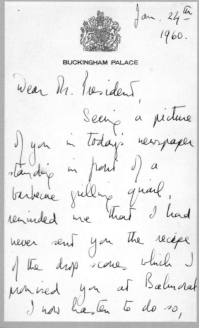

Jan. 24th 1960.

BUCKINGHAM PALACE

Dear Mr. President,

Seeing a picture of you in today's newspaper standing in front of a barbecue grilling quail, reminded me that I had never sent you the recipe of the drop scones which I promised you at Balmoral. I now hasten to do so,

BARLEY-RYE BISCUITS

Barley flour, 1 cup

Rye flour, 1 cup

Baking powder, 4 teaspoons

Salt, 1 teaspoon

Milk, ¾ cup

Fat, 3 tablespoons

Sift together the dry ingredients; cut in the fat. Add liquid. Toss on lightly floured board. Roll to ¼ inch thickness. Cut. Bake in a hot oven 12 to 15 minutes.

Yield: 16 biscuits

Without Wheat, 1918, *Records of the U.S. Food Administration*

OATMEAL PEANUT BISCUITS

Oatmeal, 1 cup

Rye flour, 2 cups

Baking powder, 6 teaspoons

Salt, 2 teaspoons

Fat, 1 tablespoon

Roasted peanuts (crushed), 1 cup

Milk, ⅝ cup

Sift together the dry ingredients; cut in fat. Add crushed peanuts and milk, making a soft dough. Roll on slightly floured board to ⅜ inch thickness. Bake in hot oven about 15 minutes.

Yield: 23 biscuits

Without Wheat, 1918, *Records of the U.S. Food Administration*

COFFEE CAKE

Fat, 3 tablespoons

Molasses, ½ cup

Coffee, ¼ cup

Egg, 1

Barley or rye flour, ¼ cup

Wheat flour, ½ cup

Salt, ½ teaspoon

Baking powder, 1½ teaspoons

Cloves, ¼ teaspoon

Cinnamon, 1 teaspoon

Nutmeg, ¼ teaspoon

Raisins, ½ cup

Cream fat, add molasses, coffee, and beaten egg. Sift flour, salt, baking powder, and spices together and add gradually to liquids. Add raisins. Beat all thoroughly. Turn into greased cupcake tins and bake in a moderate oven for 25 minutes.

Yield: 12 cupcakes

Sweets without Sugar, 1918, *Records of the U.S. Food Administration*

When the Pure Food and Drugs Act of 1906 was passed, products such as Lipton's Gossip Blend Coffee began to proclaim their purity on the label, 1906. *Records of the Patent and Trademark Office.*

CORNED BEEF HASH

1 pound cooked corned beef

5 boiled potatoes

Onion to flavor

Dash of cayenne

Put ingredients through the meat grinder, using the fine knife. Grease lightly a heavy iron skillet. Pat in the hash in an even layer and cook over a low heat until a golden brown crust is formed. When brown, place a pan or lid over the skillet and turn the hash out so the browned side is on top. Slip the uncooked side in the skillet and allow this side to cook a golden brown. Turn onto a plate in the same way as when first turned and garnish with parsley.

Aunt Sammy's Radio Recipes, Records of the U.S. Department of Agriculture

COUNTRY OMELET

Sauté until just done in hot butter 1 thinly sliced, medium potato. Add and quickly cook golden, 1 sliced, medium yellow onion. Add and quickly cook crisp, about 16 dollar-sized pieces cooked, hard Virginia ham, each $1/8$ inch thick. Add all to 10-inch omelet skillet with 4 tablespoons hot butter. Add half of 8 beaten eggs; let eggs set on bottom, holding vegetables and ham; add salt, pepper, rest of eggs. Cook, tilting pan to side, pushing in sides of omelet with spatula to let eggs run under and set on bottom. Set top under hot broiler. Serve warm or cold, in wedges.

Serves: 6 to 8

Richard Nixon Presidential Library and Museum

EGGS IN POTATO NESTS

Mashed potatoes, 4 cups, seasoned
  with salt and pepper

Eggs, 6

Grease a large baking dish. Make six "nests" of
the mashed potatoes; break an egg into the center of each nest; sprinkle with salt and pepper.
Set the baking dish in a pan of hot water and
bake in a moderate oven until the egg is of the
desired hardness.

Yield: 6 servings

Potato Possibilities, ca. 1917–20, *Records of the U.S. Food
Administration*

Opposite: "Corned Beef Hash packed by Richmond Abattoir" label, 1918. *Records of the Patent
and Trademark Office. Background:* This 1910 picture of workers packing chipped beef in a factory is part of a collection of photographs taken by inspectors to fulfill the Meat Inspection Act
of 1906. *Records of the Bureau of Animal Industry. Above:* This 1916 French-language poster from
World War I proudly proclaims, "I am a brave war hen—I eat little and produce much." *Naval
Records Collection of the Office of Naval Records and Library.*

QUEEN'S DROP SCONES

4 teacups flour

4 tablespoons caster sugar

2 teacups milk

2 whole eggs

2 teaspoons bi-carbonate soda

3 teaspoons cream of tartar

2 tablespoons melted butter

Beat eggs, sugar, and about half the milk together, add flour, and mix well together adding remainder of milk as required, also bi-carbonate and cream of tartar, fold in melted butter.

Enough for 16 people

Editor's note: Caster (or castor) sugar is a very fine sugar with grains small enough to fit through a sugar "caster" or sprinkler. In the United States, we call this type of sugar "superfine."

Dwight D. Eisenhower Presidential Library and Museum

Queen Elizabeth II and President Eisenhower participate in the ceremonies marking the opening of the Saint Lawrence Seaway in Canada, June 26, 1959. *Dwight D. Eisenhower Presidential Library and Museum.*

POTATO PANCAKES

Mashed potatoes, 1 cup

Egg, 1

Barley flour, ½ cup

Salt, 1 teaspoon

Baking powder, 1 teaspoon

Sift together the flour, baking powder, and salt. Add beaten egg to mashed potatoes. Add flour to potato mixture. Fry on hot griddle.

Yield: 15 pancakes

Potato Possibilities, ca. 1917–20,
Records of the U.S. Food Administration

ONE-EGG BARLEY MUFFINS

Barley flour, 2 cups
Baking powder, 5 teaspoons
Salt, ½ teaspoon
Egg, 1
Milk, 1 cup
Molasses, 2 tablespoons
Melted fat, 1 tablespoon

Mix and sift dry ingredients. Beat egg; add it to milk and molasses. Stir liquid mixture into dry ingredients. Add melted fat. Stir quickly. Pour into well-greased muffin tins and bake in moderate oven 30 to 35 minutes.

Substitutes for 2 cups barley flour:
2 cups buckwheat flour, or
1 cup barley flour and 1 cup ground rolled oats, or
1½ cups rice flour

Yield: 12 muffins

*Without Wheat, 1918, Records of the
U.S. Food Administration*

CARROT MARMALADE

Carrots, 1½ pounds (5½ cups chopped)	Salt, ½ teaspoon
Lemons, 3	Corn syrup, white, 4½ cups
Oranges, 2	

Wash and scrub carrots, blanch in wire basket in boiling water for 4 to 5 minutes, cold dip, scrape, and cut into small pieces. Place in double boiler, add lemon juice and salt and cook for an hour. Add finely cut rind from oranges, the orange pulp and syrup; boil slowly until thick. Pour into hot glasses, partially seal and sterilize 10 minutes. Tighten seal. Let cool. Label and store.

Yield: 14 glasses

Sweets without Sugar, 1918, Records of the U.S. Food Administration

PEACH CONSERVE

Peaches, 3 pounds (10 medium sized)	Salt, ⅓ teaspoon
Corn syrup, 1½ cups	Water, ½ cup
Raisins, seeded, ½ cup	Walnuts, ½ pound
Oranges, small, 2 (rind and juice)	Dates, 1 cup

Remove skins from peaches, stone and cut into pieces. Add syrup, raisins, salt, finely chopped oranges and water. Cook slowly for about one hour or until the consistency of marmalade. Add nuts five minutes before removing from the fire. Pack in hot jars. Partially seal. Sterilize 10 minutes. Tighten seal. Let cool. Label and store. One cup of dates may be cooked with conserve, if desired.

A pear conserve can be made by substituting pears for the peaches in the above recipe and adding the juice of half a lemon.

Sweets without Sugar, 1918, Records of the U.S. Food Administration

PLUM CONSERVE

Sweet plums, 1 pound (2 dozen)

Raisins, ⅓ pound (1 cup)

Oranges, 2

Corn syrup, dark, ⅓ cup

Salt, ¼ teaspoon

Nut meats, ⅛ pound (¼ cup)

Wash plums; stone and cut in pieces; add seeded raisins, orange pulp, and peel, cut very fine, corn syrup, salt, and water; simmer until it has the consistency of marmalade (about 1½ hours of slow cooking). Add nuts 5 minutes before removing from fire. Pack in hot jars. Partially seal. Sterilize 10 minutes. Tighten seal.

For sour plums, more syrup must be added.

Yield: 1½ pints of conserve

Sweets without Sugar, 1918, Records of the U.S. Food Administration

GOOSEBERRY JAM

4 pounds gooseberries

4 pounds sugar

Remove the stems, or the "tops and tails," from the gooseberries. Wash the berries, crush, and cook until fairly tender. Add the sugar and continue cooking until thick. If the berries are ripe and not too acid, three-fourths as much sugar as fruit can be used. Pour into hot sterile glasses or jars and seal, label, and store in a cool place.

*Aunt Sammy's Radio Recipes, Records of the
U.S. Department of Agriculture*

This detail is from a World War II *Little Americans* poster, encouraging citizens of all ages to do their part for the war effort, ca. 1918. *Records of the U.S. Food Administration.*

JFK'S FAVORITE WAFFLES

½ cup butter

1 tablespoon sugar

2 egg yolks

⅞ cup milk, or one cup
   buttermilk

1 cup and one tablespoon of
   sifted cake flour

1 pinch salt

2 stiff beaten egg whites

4 tablespoons baking powder

Cream butter and sugar, add egg yolks. Beat. Add flour and milk alternately. This may be done at any time. When ready to bake, fold in egg whites, and add baking powder. Mixture should be thick and fluffy. Bake and serve with hot maple syrup and melted butter.

John F. Kennedy Presidential Library and Museum

POTATO SAUSAGES

Mashed potatoes, 1 cup

Meat, fish, or nuts, 1 cup
   (chopped)

Egg, well beaten, 1

Pepper, ⅛ teaspoon

Salt pork, bacon or drippings

Chopped onion, 1 tablespoon

Salt, 1½ teaspoons

Mix the mashed potatoes, seasonings and chopped meat. Add ½ of the beaten egg. To the other half of the egg, add 1½ tablespoons water. Form the potato mixture into cakes, like sausages; dip into cornmeal; dip into egg to which water has been added; dip again in cornmeal. Fry in drippings, or brown in oven with bacon.

Yield: 12 "sausages"

Potato Possibilities, ca. 1917–20, *Records of the U.S. Food Administration*

Opposite, top: "Elk Brand Boneless Breakfast Bacon" label, 1916. Opposite, bottom: This "Grains of Health" drink label from 1906 claims to be "more wholesome and nourishing than any of the Cereal Drinks, Tea, Coffee and Cocoa," but it is unclear what it is, much less what type and amount of nutrients it offers. Records of the Patent and Trademark Office.

SCRAPPLE

Select 3 pounds of very bony pieces of pork or pork and beef mixed, if preferred. A hog's head may be used for making scrapple. For each pound of bony meat, use about a quart of water and simmer until the meat drops from the bone. Remove the bone, taking care to get out all the tiny pieces. Chop the meat into small pieces. There should be about 2 quarts of broth left. If necessary, add water to make this quantity. Bring the broth to the boiling point, slowly add 2 cups of corn meal, and cook the mixture until it is like a thick mush, stirring almost constantly. Add the chopped meat, salt, and any other seasoning desired. Add onion juice, sage, and thyme, if desired. Pour the hot scrapple into dampened oblong enamelware pans. Let stand until cold and firm. Slice and brown in a hot skillet. If the scrapple is rich with fat, no more fat is needed for frying.

Aunt Sammy's Radio Recipes, Records of the U.S. Department of Agriculture

BREAKFAST APPLES

Core and peel apples, place in baking dish. Force sausage meat into cored holes and place small mound of it firmly on top of each apple. Bake until sausage and apples are done. Serve with egg poached in the usual manner.

Massachusetts Writers' Project, 1935–40, Records of the Work Projects Administration

BREAD

Wheat is one of the very few foods we can ship successfully. From now until harvest we must SAVE, SAVE, SAVE, in order to keep up our shipments to the other side. Every day we must put aside more wheat for our boys over there. Do not be satisfied with a little saving. Do all you can.

Wheatless does not mean breadless, nor cakeless, nor even pieless. You can use other flours. There are corn, rice, potatoes, barley, and oaten flours from which to choose. All you need is some reliable recipes and a little practice to have good and wholesome wheatless meals.

Do not use too much hot bread, but try some of the loaves of bread made with baking powder, and be sure to cook them as long as directed.

Wheat is not more wholesome than other cereals, only more fashionable. Let us have a new summer fashion—THE WHEATLESS.

Without Wheat, 1918, Records of the U.S. Food Administration

Opposite: Detail of The World Cry Food…Keep the Home Garden Growing poster, ca. 1918. Records of the U.S. Food Administration.

BAKING POWDER BISCUITS

4 pounds flour	1 pound, 10 ounces fat
4 teaspoons salt	1½ quarts milk
⅞ cup baking powder, phosphate	½ to 1 cup table fat, melted

1. Sift flour, salt, and baking powder together twice.
2. Cut in fat very lightly.
3. Add milk gradually, handling as little as possible.
4. Roll or pat dough to ½-inch thickness and cut with 2½-inch floured cutter.
5. Brush with melted table fat.
6. Bake at 425°F, 12 to 15 minutes.

Yield: 100 biscuits

School Lunch Recipes for 100, 1946, Bureau of Human Nutrition and Home Economics

BARLEY TEA BREAD

Barley flour, 2 cups	Egg, 1
Baking powder, 5 teaspoons	English walnut, pecan, or hickory nut meats, 1 cup
Salt, 1 teaspoon	Ground rolled oats, 1 cup
Sugar, ½ cup	
Milk, 1 cup	

Sift together the flour, baking powder, salt, and sugar; add ground rolled oats. Add the milk, the egg well beaten, and the nut meats. Place in a well-greased pan and let rise ½ hour. Bake about 1 hour in a moderate oven. Rye flour may be substituted for the barley flour if desired.

Yield: 1 loaf 4 x 10 inches and 1 loaf 2½ x 4 inches

Without Wheat, 1918, Records of the U.S. Food Administration

BREAD

BASIC DINNER ROLLS or PARKER HOUSE ROLLS

1 package yeast, active dry or compressed

¼ cup warm water

2 eggs, plus enough scalded and cooled milk to make 2 cups liquid

¼ pound melted butter or margarine

1½ teaspoons salt

½ cup sugar

6 cups regular all-purpose flour

Sprinkle yeast into large bowl, add warm water, and stir until dissolved. Add eggs, milk, butter, salt, and sugar and stir until well blended. Stir in 3 cups of the flour, beating until smooth after each cup is added. Stir in the fourth cup of flour—beat until dough is smooth and elastic. Stir in the fifth cup of flour to make stiff dough. Measure the sixth cup of flour and sprinkle half of it on a board.

Turn the dough out onto the heavily floured board and with well-floured hands, knead dough until it is smooth and elastic (about 5 minutes), using the remaining flour as needed. Place dough into a well-buttered bowl and butter the top lightly. Cover and let rise in a warm place until almost doubled in bulk (about 1½ to 2 hours).

When dough has almost doubled, punch it down, squeezing the air bubbles out with your hands. Divide dough into four parts, wrap each in plastic film and refrigerate until chilled. (You can eliminate this last step, but the rolls are much easier to shape with chilled dough.)

Using one piece of the chilled dough at a time, roll dough ¼ inch thick; cut 2½ inch circles. With dull edge of knife, crease just off center. Brush with butter, fold large part over small; press folded edge firmly.

Arrange rolls on greased baking sheet. Let rise in warm place until almost double in size.

Bake in hot oven 425°F for about 10 minutes or until browned.

For especially tender, crusted rolls, you can brush the tops with melted butter before baking.

Richard Nixon Presidential Library and Museum

Background: This woman in Mobile, Alabama, hangs posters on her fence, exhorting Americans to save wheat for those fighting abroad, 1918. *Herbert Hoover Presidential Library and Museum.*

BOSTON BROWN BREAD

1 cup corn meal	¾ cup molasses
1 cup rye meal	2 cups sour milk and 1½ teaspoons soda,
1 cup Graham flour	or 1¾ cups sweet milk and
1 teaspoon salt	4 teaspoons baking powder

Mix and sift the dry ingredients; add the molasses and the milk. Beat the mixture thoroughly. Pour the batter into a greased tin can or mold until it is about three-fourths full. Cover and steam for 3½ hours. Remove the cover, and bake the bread in a moderate oven for ½ hour to dry it off. If the bread seems likely to crumble, loop a clean string around the loaf and cut slices by pulling the ends of the string.

Aunt Sammy's Radio Recipes, Records of the U.S. Department of Agriculture

LBJ'S SPOON BREAD

"Spoon bread was one of Lyndon's mother's delightful dishes," says Mrs. Lyndon B. Johnson, *"With a salad (fruit or green) and meat, it makes the perfect lunch."*

3 cups of sweet milk	Butter the size of a walnut, melted
3 eggs	3 level teaspoons baking powder
1 scant cup of corn meal	1 level teaspoon salt

Stir corn meal into 2 cups of milk and let mixture come to a boil, making a mush. Add the remaining milk and well-beaten eggs. Stir in salt, baking powder, and melted butter. Bake 30 minutes at 350˚F.

Lyndon Baines Johnson Presidential Library and Museum

Background: Russian wheat field where USDA plant explorers found wheat varieties from which they later bred the disease-resistant wheat that saved the wheat-growing industry in the West, undated. *Records of the Office of the Secretary of Agriculture.* *Opposite, inset: Our Good Earth…Keep it Ours,* poster, by John Stewart Curry, 1942. *Publications of the U.S. Government.*

BREAD

LADY BIRD JOHNSON'S POPOVERS

1 cup of sifted flour

1 cup of milk

2 eggs, beaten

¼ teaspoon of salt

2 tablespoons of shortening
(melted)

Mix and sift flour and salt. Combine eggs, milk, and shortening; gradually add to flour mixture, beating about one minute or until batter is smooth. Fill greased sizzling hot pans three-quarters full and bake in very hot oven (450°F) about 20 minutes. Reduce heat to moderate (350°F) and continue baking for 15 or 20 minutes.

Lyndon Baines Johnson Presidential Library and Museum

Our Good Earth
...Keep It Ours

BUY WAR BONDS
"Make Every Market Day **BOND** Day"

LBJ RANCH HUSH PUPPIES

2 cups white corn meal

¼ cup butter

1 teaspoon baking powder

1 tablespoon salt

3 tablespoons sugar

3½ cups boiling water

Over heat, combine corn meal, baking powder, and salt and add slowly to 3½ cups boiling water, stirring briskly.

As soon as mixture is smooth, remove from heat and stir in butter. Cool.

Shape into "fingers" and fry in 2 inches hot fat (375°F) until golden brown. Drain on absorbent paper.

Makes about three dozen hush puppies

Lyndon Baines Johnson Presidential Library and Museum

PRESIDENT REAGAN'S MONKEY BREAD

½ ounce yeast or 1 package
    dry yeast
1 to 1¼ cups milk
3 eggs
3 tablespoons sugar
1 tablespoon salt
3½ cups flour
6 ounces butter, room
    temperature
½ pound melted butter
Two 9-inch ring molds

In bowl, mix yeast with part of milk until dissolved. Add 2 eggs, beat. Mix in dry ingredients. Add remaining milk a little at a time, mixing thoroughly. Cut in butter until blended. Knead dough, let rise 1 to 1½ hours until double in size. Knead again, let rise 40 minutes.

Roll dough onto floured board, shape into log. Cut log into 28 pieces of equal size. Shape each piece of dough into ball, roll in melted butter. Use half of the pieces in each of the buttered, floured molds. Place 7 balls in each mold, leaving space between. Place remaining balls on top, spacing evenly. Let dough rise in mold. Brush tops with remaining egg. Bake in preheated oven at 375°F until golden brown. Approximately 15 minutes.

Ronald Reagan Presidential Library and Museum

Above: After the introduction of enriched white bread to the market, the owner of the New York Bakery in Utica wrote to the Office of Defense, requesting information for putting Vitamin B in rye bread, 1942. *Records of the Agricultural Marketing Service.*

HOT WATER GINGERBREAD

Fat, 3 tablespoons

Boiling water, ½ cup

Molasses, 1 cup

Ginger, 2 teaspoons

Salt, ½ teaspoon

Soda, 1 teaspoon

Barley flour, 2½ cups

Melt the fat by adding the boiling water; add molasses. Sift together the flour, spice, salt, and soda. Add liquid gradually to the sifted dry ingredients. Beat vigorously. Pour into greased shallow pans and bake about 25 minutes in a moderate oven.

1 cup ground rolled oats may be substituted for 1 cup barley flour.

Yield: 3 cakes, 4 x 6 inches; 12 servings

Without Wheat, 1918, Records of the U.S. Food Administration

....

CORN BREAD

2 cups corn meal

2 cups sour milk

½ teaspoon soda

2 teaspoons baking powder

2 teaspoons salt

2 eggs

2 tablespoons melted butter

Sift the dry ingredients. Add the milk and the soda which has been dissolved in a small quantity of hot water. Add the well-beaten eggs and the butter. Pour into a very hot, well-buttered pan. Bake from 40 to 50 minutes at a temperature from 400°F to 450°F.

Aunt Sammy's Radio Recipes, U.S. Department of Agriculture

OATEN LOAF

Ground oatmeal, 2 cups	Egg, 1
Baking powder, 4 teaspoons	Milk, 1 cup
Salt, 1 teaspoon	(½ cup raisins may be added, if desired)

Mix and sift dry ingredients; beat egg and add to milk. Add the liquid ingredients gradually to the dry ingredients. Pour into greased bread pans. Allow to rise 20 minutes. Bake in a moderate oven about 35 minutes.

Yield: 1 loaf

Without Wheat, 1918, *Records of the U.S. Food Administration*

....

PEANUT BUTTER LOAF

Barley flour, 1 cup	Peanut butter, ½ cup
Rye flour, 1 cup	Milk, 1 cup
Baking powder, 4 teaspoons	Salt, 1 teaspoon
Sugar, ¼ cup	

Sift together the dry ingredients. Add peanut butter, working in with tips of fingers, or knife. Add milk. Turn into greased bread pan. Allow to stand 20 minutes. Bake in a moderate oven about 1 hour.

Yield: 1 loaf

Without Wheat, 1918, *Records of the U.S. Food Administration*

Background: Men loading durum wheat in Siberia, undated. *Records of the Bureau of Plant Industry, Soils, and Agricultural Engineering. Opposite, top: Save a loaf a week—help win the war* poster, ca. 1918. *Records of the U.S. Food Administration. Opposite, bottom: Men and Wheat* mural, by Joe Jones, painted on the post office in Seneca, Kansas, as part of the New Deal, 1939. *Records of the Public Buildings Service.*

POTATO STEAMED BREAD

Mashed potatoes, 2 cups
Barley flour, 1 cup
Cornmeal, 1 cup
Water or milk, ¾ cup
Soda, ½ teaspoon

Baking powder,
 1 teaspoon
Salt, 1 teaspoon
Molasses, ¾ cup

Mix and sift barley flour, cornmeal, soda, baking powder, and salt. Combine mashed potatoes, milk, and molasses and add to the dry ingredients. Stir well; fill greased molds two-thirds full. Grease covers and cover tightly. Steam three hours.

Yield: 6 one-half pound baking powder tins

Potato Possibilities, ca. 1917–20, *Records of the U.S. Food Administration*

STEAMED BROWN BREAD

Ground oatmeal, 1 cup
Cornmeal, 1 cup
Barley flour, 1 cup
Baking powder, 1 teaspoon

Salt, 1 teaspoon
Soda, ⅜ teaspoon
Molasses, ¾ cup
Milk, 1¾ cups

Mix and sift dry ingredients. Add molasses and milk and mix thoroughly. Grease molds and covers. Fill two-thirds full of mixture. Cover and steam 3 hours.

Yield: 5 one-half pound baking powder tins

Without Wheat, 1918, *Records of the U.S. Food Administration*

SNACKS

If every Cosmopolitan *family does its bit, the million households in which this magazine is read can alone save wheat and meat enough to nourish a million fighting men. The need for food conservation is not "Fool conversation." Two sorts of submarines threaten the Allies—the U-boat isn't a whit more effective than the slacker garbage-pail.*

If each of you takes care of the little wastes in your home, the big war will soon take care of itself. Women of the United States are the final arbiters of this appalling conflict.

As they write their market-lists, they determine the fate of the state and its foes. Cook the Kaiser's goose on your own stoves.

Victory over there is being weighed upon grocers' scales here.

The flag out front signifies nothing unless it's also hanging in the ice-box. Whoever pampers special tastes hampers the army—dines upon the very Stars and Stripes.

We have challenged the dreadest military force in all annals, and we shall fail ignominiously and be marred eternally if our appetites aren't patriots. Stand in the bread-lines of defense—serve ornate and lavish meals now, and you serve the enemy.

Every time you pass the plate for a second helping, Berlin thanks you.

Democracy is equally menaced by gluttony and Germany. Don't crucify Civilization on a cross of knives and forks.

God help a people that stints the field-kitchen to stuff the home larder. It's a shoddy and pinchbeck loyalty that sends sons to the battle-front and won't spare a crust to comrades in arms.

France, England, and Italy can provide as many troops as we'll provision. Extravagant Americans are holding whole regiments from the trenches. Stop eating soldiers!

—Herbert Kaufman, column in *Cosmopolitan* magazine, 1918. *Distributed by the U.S. Food Administration*

Opposite: Detail of *Field Marshal "Potato Pete"* poster, undated. *Records of the Office of Government Reports.*

LAURA BUSH'S GUACAMOLE

8 ripe avocados

4 lemons, juiced

7 shallots, finely chopped

1 jalapeño pepper, seeded and finely chopped

½ bunch cilantro, finely chopped

1 teaspoon black pepper

1 tablespoon salt

Halve and pit avocados and scoop out flesh into a bowl. Mash to desired consistency and mix in remaining ingredients. Cover with plastic wrap and refrigerate for about an hour before serving. Serve with tortilla chips.

George W. Bush Presidential Library

BARBARA BUSH'S MEXICAN MOUND–A Great Bush Favorite!

Easy to make—loved by all who love Mexican food. Ingredients easy to keep in the house. Children or guests can all help with chopping or grating. It's fun!

A – Package of corn chips

B – 2 pounds ground meat

C – Taco seasoning mix

D – 1 cup grated yellow cheese

E – 1 or 2 small chopped onions (not minced)

F – 10 chopped ripe black olives

G – 1 chopped tomato

H – 1 cup sour cream

I – Lettuce (a cup shredded)

J – 1 medium can of frozen avocado dip

Follow instructions on taco seasoning mix for browning meat. I serve this meal in my kitchen—a big pot of meat simmering on the stove, a wooden salad bowl of corn chips, and seven bowls (D through J) of the remaining ingredients around the table. Start with a mound of corn chips, a spoon of piping hot meat, cheese, etc.

George Bush Presidential Library and Museum

SNACKS

CHEESE STRAWS

1 cup flour	1 cup grated cheese
½ teaspoon salt	¹⁄₁₆ teaspoon cayenne
¼ cup fat	3 tablespoons water

Cut the flour, salt, cayenne, fat, and one-half of the cheese together with a biscuit cutter until the mass is well blended. Add the water and mix well. Toss on a slightly floured board and roll 2 or 3 times until the dough is smooth. Sprinkle on one-half of the remainder of the cheese and roll again. Repeat this until all the cheese is used. Roll the mass out until about ¼ inch thick. Cut into strips ½ inch wide and 6 inches long. Place the strips on a baking sheet and bake until a delicate brown, in a hot oven, about 400°F.

Aunt Sammy's Radio Recipes, Records of the U.S. Department of Agriculture

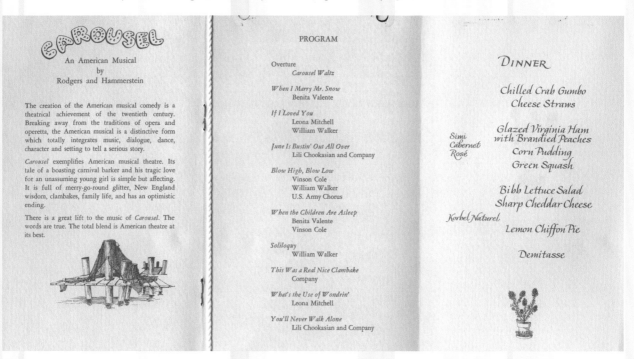

Formal dinner menu for Chancellor Helmut Schmidt of West Germany, featuring "Cheese Straws," 1977. *Jimmy Carter Presidential Library and Museum.*

POTATO CORNMEAL CRISPS

Cornmeal, ½ cup   Fat, 1 tablespoon

Salt, ½ teaspoon   Mashed potatoes, ½ cup

Sift the cornmeal and salt; cut in the fat. Add mashed potatoes, making a dough which can be rolled very thin. Cut into diamond shapes and bake in a quick oven until golden brown. If desired, after rolling cut the dough, sprinkle with grated cheese and paprika, making cheese straws.

Yield: 50 wafers, 2 x 2 inches

Without Wheat, 1918, *Records of the U.S. Food Administration*

LADY BIRD JOHNSON'S CHEESE WAFERS

1 cup margarine or soft butter   1 teaspoon cayenne pepper

2 cups flour   ½ teaspoon salt

8 ounces sharp cheddar cheese, grated   2 cups Rice Krispies cereal

Cut butter into flour, add cheese and seasonings, fold in cereal. Drop by small rounds on ungreased cookie sheet and flatten with spoon.

Bake at 350°F for about 12–15 minutes, depending on oven (careful not to get too brown).

Yield: Approximately 5 dozen wafers

Lyndon Baines Johnson Presidential Library and Museum

Top: According to this 1918 display from World War I, "A Golden Opportunity to Show Your Patriotism" is to use cornmeal instead of wheat. *Herbert Hoover Presidential Library and Museum. Bottom:* Lady Bird Johnson, President Lyndon B. Johnson, and Yuki sitting near the Pedernales River, 1967. *Lyndon Baines Johnson Presidential Library and Museum.*

"PLAINS SPECIAL" CHEESE RING

1 pound grated sharp cheese

1 cup finely chopped nuts

1 cup mayonnaise

1 small onion, finely grated

Black pepper

Dash cayenne

Strawberry preserves,
    optional

Combine all ingredients except preserves, season to taste with pepper. Mix well and place in a 5- or 6-cup lightly greased ring mold. Refrigerate until firm for several hours or overnight.

To serve, unmold, and if desired, fill center with strawberry preserves, or serve plain with crackers.

Jimmy Carter Presidential Library and Museum

PRESIDENT AND LAURA BUSH'S DEVILED EGGS

12 large eggs, boiled hard and peeled

1 tablespoon (plus) soft butter

1 tablespoon (plus) mayonnaise

1 tablespoon Dijon mustard

½ teaspoon Yucatan Sunshine habañero pepper sauce

Salt to taste

Cut eggs in half and set aside. Put egg yolks in food processor and add all ingredients. Process for 20 seconds or until mixture has blended. Check for taste and increase mustard, salt, or habañero sauce, if desired. Place mixture in piping bag with star tip and pipe into egg halves. Sprinkle with paprika and chopped parsley. Chill for about an hour before serving.

The Bushes used Yucatan Sunshine habañero pepper sauce while living in Texas, so the White House chef incorporated it into a variety of recipes. It can be substituted with Tabasco sauce.

George W. Bush Presidential Library

ONIONS FRIED in DEEP FAT

Remove the outer skin of the onions and slice very thin. Dip the slices into a thin batter made of 1 cup flour, 1 cup milk, 1 egg, and ¼ teaspoon salt, and drain well.

Use lard or other cooking fat for frying. Have a frying kettle about half full of hot fat. Be careful that the fat is not so hot that it smokes. Drop a small piece of bread into the fat. If it browns in about 1 minute, the fat is just right for the onions. Put the slices of onion in a wire basket or sieve, so they can be easily removed from the fat. Lower the sieve or basket into the hot fat and let the onions fry until they are golden brown. Drain the onions on absorbent paper.

Onions fixed this way are very good with steak. They will keep crisp for some days.

Aunt Sammy's Radio Recipes, Records of the U.S. Department of Agriculture

Above: After the Pure Food and Drugs Act passed in 1906, catsup, such as this, was investigated for contamination, 1909. *Records of the Food and Drug Administration. Opposite:* "Heinz's Catsup" label, 1883. *Records of the Patent and Trademark Office.*

SNACKS

28

OYSTER COCKTAIL

1 pint raw oysters

6 tablespoons tomato catsup

3 tablespoons lemon juice or vinegar

12 drops Tabasco sauce

½ teaspoon salt

2 tablespoons chopped celery

1 tablespoon Worcestershire sauce

2 tablespoons grated horseradish

Mix all the ingredients except the oysters. Chill. Place the cold oysters in cocktail glasses. Add the sauce just before serving.

Aunt Sammy's Radio Recipes, Records of the U.S. Department of Agriculture

POTATO BALLS

Potatoes, small, 5
Egg yolk, 1
Fat or olive oil, 1½ tablespoons
Parsley, chopped, 3 teaspoons
Salt, ½ teaspoon
Pepper, ⅛ teaspoon
Cheese, grated, ¼ cup
Egg, ½, for dipping
Cornmeal, ¼ cup (for crumbling)

Cook potatoes in boiling, salted water; drain and mash; add beaten egg yolk, cheese, parsley, salt, and pepper and mix thoroughly. Let stand on board until cold (about 15 minutes). Roll into small balls; dip in cornmeal, egg, and again in cornmeal. Sauté in olive oil or fat in frying pan until golden brown.

Yield: 4 servings (3 balls apiece)

Potato Possibilities, ca. 1917–20, *Records of the U.S. Food Administration*

STUFFED CELERY

Cut the celery into pieces convenient for handling. Fill the hollow of the celery stalks with cream cheese mixed with chopped pimiento, green pepper, and chopped nuts. Serve on the plate with another salad or as a relish.

Aunt Sammy's Radio Recipes, Records of the U.S. Department of Agriculture

FRENCH FRIED POTATOES

Peel and cut potatoes lengthwise into strips about ½ inch thick. Rinse the strips in cold running water, and soak for 2 or 3 hours in cold water to remove as much starch as possible. Remove from the water, and pat with a clean dry cloth to absorb the surface moisture. Heat a kettle of deep fat hot enough to brown a small piece of bread in 60 seconds. Fry about a cupful of potatoes at a time. Remove them from the fat when golden brown, drain on clean absorbent paper, and sprinkle with salt. Serve at once while hot and crisp.

Aunt Sammy's Radio Recipes, Records of the U.S. Department of Agriculture

Top: President Clinton visits the Varsity Diner in Atlanta, 1996. *William J. Clinton Presidential Library and Museum.* *Bottom:* President Barack Obama orders lunch at Five Guys in Washington, DC, during an unannounced lunch outing May 29, 2009. *Official White House Photo by Pete Souza.*

SOUPS

Dear Lynn:

Your nice letter to the President has been received and he has asked me to tell you he certainly appreciates your friendly thought in writing.

In answer to your inquiry, one of the President's favorite dishes is fish chowder. With the thought that you might like to have it, I am enclosing the recipe. I am also sending along a photograph of the President which comes with his best wishes.

Sincerely,

Ralph A. Dungan
(Special Assistant to President Kennedy)

Typewritten letter to Lynn Jennings, St. Louis, Missouri, from President John F. Kennedy's special assistant, May 18, 1961. *John F. Kennedy Presidential Library and Museum.*

Opposite: President John F. Kennedy with his son, John, Jr., on the beach at Newport, Rhode Island, 1963. *John F. Kennedy Presidential Library and Museum.*

ACORN SQUASH AND LEEK SOUP WITH TOASTED PECANS

2 acorn squash	½ cup toasted chopped pecans
1 large leek	1 tablespoon butter
1 quart chicken stock	2 tablespoons chopped chives

Cut acorn squash in half and bake in a 350°F oven for 30–45 minutes or until tender. Remove from the oven and cool. Scoop out the seeds and discard them. Scoop out the flesh from the skin. Dice the leek into small pieces and wash. Sauté the leek in butter until tender, then add squash and about two-thirds of the chicken stock. Stir everything together and cook. Add additional chicken stock if too thick. Put the soup in a blender and mix until smooth. Again, add more chicken stock if too thick. Season with salt and pepper. Garnish hot soup with chopped toasted pecans and chives.

William J. Clinton Presidential Library and Museum

CREAM OF QUAHOG SOUP

30 quahogs	1 tablespoon of butter
¼ cup quahog juice	1 tablespoon of flour
2 slices of onion	1 cup of cream
1 quart of milk	Minced parsley
1 teaspoon of sugar	

Method: Chop quahogs very fine, place in double boiler with onion and clam (quahog) juice. Cook for five minutes. Add milk and sugar. Let stand, but do not cook. Blend butter and flour and stir in. Cook three minutes. Strain and add cream. Serve in bouillon cups with minced parsley on top.

Records of the Work Projects Administration

LAURA BUSH'S WILD MUSHROOM SOUP

1½ quarts chicken stock

1 pint heavy cream

Butter

1 tablespoon flour

Salt and pepper

½ pound wild mushrooms
(chanterelle or yellow fot)

½ pound shiitaki mushrooms

½ pound cremini mushrooms

1 leek (white only, finely diced)

1 small sweet onion (finely diced)

2 garlic cloves, chopped

½ teaspoon fresh thyme, chopped

Cook leek and onion over low heat in a small covered stock pot with a little butter. Do not color. Clean and chop all the mushrooms and add to leek and onion. Add chopped garlic and thyme. Continue to cook and add more butter, if necessary, until the mushrooms are cooked. Sprinkle in a level tablespoon of flour and mix well. Add 1 quart of chicken stock and bring to a simmer for 20 minutes and keep stirring. Add one cup of cream and cook for five more minutes. Put the soup in a blender and purée the soup. Leave it a little chunky and return it to the stove. Add salt and pepper, as well as more cream and chicken stock if necessary.

Makes 6 servings

George W. Bush Presidential Library

Wanna Keep 'Em Healthy? poster, ca. 1932–37.
Records of the Office of Government Reports.

OBAMA FAMILY CHILI RECIPE

1 large onion, chopped
1 green pepper, chopped
Several cloves of garlic, chopped
1 tablespoon olive oil
1 pound ground turkey or beef
¼ teaspoon ground cumin
¼ teaspoon ground oregano
¼ teaspoon ground turmeric
¼ teaspoon ground basil
1 tablespoon chili powder
3 tablespoons red wine vinegar
Several tomatoes, depending
   on size, chopped
1 can red kidney beans

Sauté onions, green pepper, and garlic in olive oil until soft. Add ground meat and brown. Combine spices together into a mixture, then add to ground meat. Add red wine vinegar. Add tomatoes and let simmer, until tomatoes cook down. Add kidney beans and cook for a few more minutes. Serve over white or brown rice. Garnish with grated cheddar cheese, onions, and sour cream.

Courtesy of the White House

Above: President Barack Obama with First Lady Michelle Obama and daughters Sasha and Malia hike on Cadillac Mountain at Acadia National Park in Maine, July 16, 2010. *Official White House Photo by Pete Souza. Opposite:* Sen. Lyndon Johnson and Lady Bird Johnson on the Pedernales River, 1959. *Lyndon Baines Johnson Presidential Library and Museum.*

SOUPS

PRESIDENT JOHNSON'S PEDERNALES RIVER CHILI

4 pounds chili meat (coarsely ground round steak or well-trimmed chuck)

1 large onion, chopped

2 cloves garlic

1 teaspoon ground oregano

1 teaspoon comino seed

6 teaspoons chili powder (or more, if needed)

1½ cups canned whole tomatoes

2–6 generous dashes liquid hot sauce

2 cups hot water

Salt to taste. Place meat, onion, and garlic in large, heavy pan or Dutch oven. Cook until light in color. Add oregano, comino seed, chili powder, tomatoes, hot pepper sauce, salt, and hot water. Bring to a boil. Lower heat and simmer for about 1 hour. Skim off fat during cooking.

Lyndon Baines Johnson Presidential Library and Museum

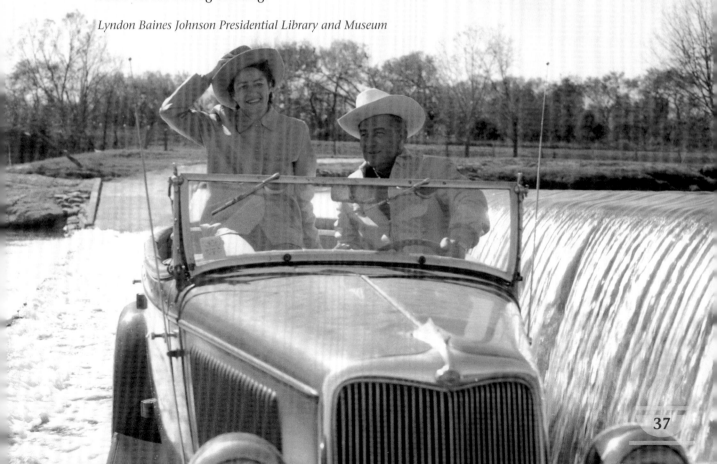

PRESIDENT KENNEDY'S NEW ENGLAND FISH CHOWDER

2 pounds haddock	1 bay leaf, crumbled
2 ounces salt pork, diced	1 quart milk
2 onions, sliced	2 tablespoons butter
4 large potatoes, diced	1 teaspoon salt
1 cup chopped celery	Freshly ground black pepper

Simmer haddock in 2 cups of water for 15 minutes. Drain. Reserve broth. Remove bones from fish. Sauté diced pork until crisp, remove and set aside. Sauté onions in pork fat until golden brown. Add fish, potatoes, celery, bay leaf, salt, and pepper. Pour in fish broth plus enough boiling water to make 3 cups of liquid. Simmer for 30 minutes. Add milk and butter and simmer for 5 minutes. Serve chowder sprinkled with pork dice.

Serves 6

John F. Kennedy Presidential Library and Museum

President Kennedy, Jacqueline Kennedy, John, Jr., Caroline, and dogs during a weekend at Hyannisport, Massachusetts, 1963. *John F. Kennedy Presidential Library and Museum.*

SOUPS

GENERAL EISENHOWER'S OLD-FASHIONED BEEF STEW

20 pounds stewing meat
  (prime round)

8 pounds small Irish potatoes

6 bunches small carrots

5 pounds small onions

15 fresh tomatoes

1 bunch bouquet garniture

3 gallons beef stock

Salt, pepper, and Accent
  (meat tenderizer)

Stew the meat until tender. Add the vegetables and bouquet garniture (thyme, bay leaves, garlic, etc. in cloth bag). When vegetables are done, strain off 2 gallons of stock from the stew and thicken slightly with beef roux. Pour back into stew and let simmer for one-half hour.

Serves 60

To adapt above recipe to average family use (6 portions), use one-tenth of the ingredients listed.

2 pounds stewing meat
 (prime round)

1 pound small Irish potatoes

1 bunch small carrots

¾ pound small onions

2 fresh tomatoes

Assorted spices

2½ pints beef stock

Salt, pepper, and Accent (meat tenderizer)

Receipt from François Baillet for "portable soup" for the Lewis and Clark expedition, 1803. *Records of the Office of the Quartermaster General.*

Cook as in above recipe, straining off 1 cup of stock from stew instead of the 2 gallons.

It must be emphasized that the recipe using these portions has not been tested.

Dwight D. Eisenhower Presidential Library and Museum

ONION WINE SOUP

¼ cup butter

5 large onions, chopped

5 cups beef broth

½ cup celery leaves

1 large potato, sliced

1 cup dry white wine

1 tablespoon vinegar

2 teaspoons sugar

1 cup light cream

1 tablespoon minced parsley

Salt and pepper

Melt butter in large saucepan. Add chopped onion and mix well. Add beef broth, celery leaves, and potato. Bring to boiling. Cover and simmer for 30 minutes. Purée mixture in a blender. Return to saucepan and blend in wine, vinegar, and sugar. Bring to boiling and simmer 5 minutes. Stir in cream, parsley, and salt and pepper to taste. Heat thoroughly but do not boil.

6 to 8 servings

Ronald Reagan Presidential Library and Museum

OX TAIL STEW

1 ox tail

2½ quarts water

4 carrots, diced

2 turnips, diced

2 onions, sliced

1 large potato, diced

2 tablespoons butter

1 teaspoon Worcestershire or
   other seasoning

Salt and pepper to taste

1 tablespoon parsley, chopped fine

Slices of lemon

Wash the ox tail, cut in short lengths, and brown it in its own fat. Cook the onions in the butter, add to the meat with 1½ quarts of the water, and simmer until the meat is tender. In the meantime, cook the carrots and turnips for 10 minutes in 1 quart of the water and add to the meat, with the water in which they cooked. Add also the potatoes, the sauce, and the salt and pepper. When the vegetables are soft, thicken the stew with a small quantity of flour mixed with a little cold water to a smooth paste. Cook until thickened. Sprinkle with the parsley and garnish with slices of lemon.

Aunt Sammy's Radio Recipes, Records of the U.S. Department of Agriculture

SOUPS

ONION SOUP au GRATIN

3 cups meat broth
6 medium-sized
  onions, chopped
½ teaspoon salt
4 tablespoons flour
2 tablespoons cold water
Pepper
Toast
Parmesan cheese

Cook the chopped onions in a small amount of water until tender. Add 2 tablespoons of fat from the meat broth or the same quantity of butter and let onions cook down in this until they are yellow. Mix them with the meat broth and salt and thicken with the flour and cold water which have been blended. Cook for a few minutes. Season with pepper as desired. Pour the soup into bowls or soup plates, place on top a round or slice of toasted bread, and sprinkle grated cheese over the bread and soup. Serve at once.

Aunt Sammy's Radio Recipes, Records of the U.S. Department of Agriculture

Posters such as this one encouraging cooks to *Know Your Onions* were commonly used during World War II to persuade citizens and soldiers to assist the war effort through food conservation and awareness, 1943. *Records of the Office of Government Reports.*

POTATO OATMEAL SOUP

Potatoes, diced, 3 cups

Boiling water, 2¼ quarts

Rolled oats, 1½ cups

Onions, chopped, 2

Bay leaf, 1

Thyme, 1 sprig

Salt, ½ tablespoon

Pepper, ¼ teaspoon

Carrots, diced, 1½ cups

Add oatmeal gradually to boiling salted water, stirring constantly. Cook 30 minutes. Add potatoes, carrots, onions, pepper, and seasonings and cook until the potatoes and carrots are soft and the soup thickened. Two cups canned tomatoes may be added, if desired.

Potato Possibilities, ca. 1917–20, *Records of the U.S. Food Administration*

CINCO DE MAYO CHILLED AVOCADO SOUP WITH SERRANO-FLAVORED CRABMEAT

3 ripe avocados
⅓ cup peeled cucumber purée
1 cup light chicken stock
1 pint fat-free buttermilk
½ pound fresh lump crabmeat (cleaned)
1 lime, juiced
1 serrano pepper (finely diced)
2 tablespoons red bell pepper (finely diced)
2 tablespoons cilantro (coarsely chopped)
Fine sea salt and fresh ground pepper (to taste)
Yucatan Sunshine habañero pepper sauce (to taste)

Cut avocados in half and remove pits. Scoop out the flesh and put in a blender, add half of the lime juice, cucumber purée, half the buttermilk and chicken stock, a pinch of salt and pepper, and a little hot pepper sauce. Pulse the blender slowly to purée everything. Add more buttermilk and chicken stock until you receive a smooth consistency. Adjust the seasoning to your taste (avocado does need some salt added). Refrigerate for an hour. Mix crabmeat with some lime juice, serrano pepper, red pepper, and pinch of salt and pepper. Ladle the soup into chilled bowls, put a tablespoon of crab mixture on top, and sprinkle with chopped cilantro to finish.

Makes 6 servings

George W. Bush Presidential Library

Opposite: Roy Carter in his oat field, Jefferson County, Tennessee, 1937. *Records of the Tennessee Valley Authority.* *Above, top*: President George W. Bush poses with members of the Los Hermanos Mora Arriaga mariachi band, who performed in the Rose Garden at the White House on Friday, May 4, 2007, during a celebration of Cinco de Mayo. *Above, bottom:* President Bush embraces band member Angelica Mora Arriaga. *George W. Bush Presidential Library.*

GENERAL EISENHOWER'S VEGETABLE SOUP

The best time to make vegetable soup is a day or so after you have had fried chicken and out of which you have saved the necks, ribs, backs, un-cooked. (The chicken is not essential, but does add something.)

Procure from the meat market a good beef soup bone—the bigger the better. It is a rather good idea to have it split down the middle so that all the marrow is exposed. In addition, buy a couple pounds of ordinary soup meat, either beef or mutton, or both.

Put all this meat, early in the morning, in a big kettle. The best kind is heavy aluminum, but a good iron pot will do almost as well. Put in also the bony parts of the chicken you have saved. Cover it with water, something on the order of 5 quarts. Add a teaspoon of salt, a bit of black pepper and, if you like, a touch of garlic (one small piece). If you don't like garlic, put in an onion. Boil all this slowly all day long. Keep on boiling till the meat has literally dropped off the bone. If your stock boils down during the day, add enough water from time to time to keep the meat covered. When the whole thing has practically disintegrated, pour out into another large kettle through a colander. Make sure that the marrow is out of the bones. Let this drain through the colander for quite awhile as much juice will drain out of the meat. (Shake the colander well to help get out all the juice).

Save a few of the better pieces of meat just to cut up a little bit in small pieces to put into your soup after it is done. Put the kettle containing the stock you now have in a very cool place, outdoors in the winter time or in the ice box; let it stand all night and the next day until you are ready to make your soup.

You will find that a hard layer of fat has formed on top of the stock which can usually be lifted off since the whole kettle full of stock has jelled. Some people like a little bit of the fat left on and some like their soup very rich and do not remove more than about half of the fat.

Put the stock back into your kettle and you are now ready to make your soup.

In a separate pan, boil slowly about a third of a teacupful of barley. This should be cooked separately since it has a habit, in a soup kettle, of settling to the bottom and if your fire should happen to get too hot, it is likely to burn. If you cannot get barley use rice, but it is a poor substitute.

One of the secrets of making good vegetable soup is not to cook any of the vegetables too long. However, it is impossible to give you an exact measure of the vegetables you should put in because some people like their vegetable soup almost as thick as stew, others like it much thinner. Moreover, sometimes you can get exactly the vegetables you want; other times you have to substitute. Where you use canned vegetables, put them in only a few minutes before taking the soup off the fire. If you use fresh ones, naturally they must be fully cooked in the soup. *Recipe continues on next page.*

The things put into the soup are about as follows:

1 quart can of canned tomatoes

½ teacupful of fresh peas. If you can't get peas, a handful of good green
  beans cut up very small can substitute.

2 normal sized potatoes, diced into cubes of about half-inch size

2 or 3 branches of good celery

1 good-sized onion (sliced)

3 nice-sized carrots, diced about the same size as potatoes

1 turnip, diced like the potatoes

½ cup of canned corn

A handful of raw cabbage cut up in small pieces

Your vegetables should not all be dumped in at once. The potatoes, for example, will cook more quickly than the carrots. Your effort must be to have them all nicely cooked, but not mushy, at about the same time.

The fire must not be too hot but the soup should keep bubbling.

When you figure the soup is about done, put in your barley which should not be fully cooked, add a tablespoonful of prepared gravy seasoning and taste for flavoring, particularly salt and pepper, and if you have it, use some onion salt, garlic salt, and celery salt. (If you cannot get the gravy seasoning, use one teaspoonful of Worcestershire sauce.)

Cut up the few bits of the meat you have saved and put about a small handful into the soup.

While you are cooking the soup do not allow the liquid to boil down too much. Add a bit of water from time to time. If your stock was good and thick when you started, you can add more water than if it was thin when you started.

As a final touch, in the springtime when nasturtiums are green and tender, you can take a few nasturtium stems, cut them up in small pieces, boil them separately as you did the barley, and add them to your soup. (About one tablespoonful after cooking.)

Dwight D. Eisenhower Presidential Library and Museum

Previous page: Gen. Dwight D. Eisenhower, commander-in-chief of the Allied Expeditionary Force, gives the order of the day to U.S. paratroopers before the first assault of the D-day invasion, June 6, 1944. *Records of the Office of the Chief Signal Officer.*

SUMMER TOMATO GAZPACHO

GAZPACHO

6 large ripe tomatoes, peeled, seeded, and coarsely chopped

2 crisp cucumbers, peeled, seeded, and coarsely chopped

1 green bell pepper, seeded, and coarsely chopped

1 medium red onion, coarsely chopped

1 cup red wine vinegar

6 large garlic cloves, minced

16 ounces tomato juice

¼ cup extra virgin olive oil

Splash of your favorite hot sauce

Salt and fresh ground pepper to taste

GARNISH

6 slices of white bread, cut into small cubes

½ cup diced cucumber

½ cup diced green pepper

½ cup diced tomato

½ cup diced red onion

In a blender, blend the ingredients on high speed for three or four minutes, until very smooth. Strain [using] a coarse strainer. Season with salt, pepper, and vinegar as needed. Keep chilled.

For the crouton garnish, heat olive oil in a sauté pan, add some fresh garlic, and cook until it is fragrant. Add the bread cubes and stir to coat. You could finish the croutons by baking in the oven (350°F) for a few minutes, until it is golden brown.

Serve the soup with the diced cucumber, tomatoes, red onion, green pepper, and the homemade croutons.

Serves 6

William J. Clinton Presidential Library and Museum

POULTRY

I do therefore invite my fellow citizens in every part of the United States, and also those who are at sea and those who are sojourning in foreign lands, to set apart and observe the last Thursday of November next, as a day of Thanksgiving and Praise to our beneficent Father who dwelleth in the Heavens. And I recommend to them that while offering up the ascriptions justly due to Him for such singular deliverances and blessings, they do also, with humble penitence for our national perverseness and disobedience, commend to His tender care all those who have become widows, orphans, mourners or sufferers in the lamentable civil strife in which we are unavoidably engaged, and fervently implore the interposition of the Almighty Hand to heal the wounds of the nation and to restore it as soon as may be consistent with the Divine purposes to the full enjoyment of peace, harmony, tranquility and Union.

President Abraham Lincoln's Thanksgiving Day Proclamation, October 3, 1863. *General Records of the U.S. Government*

Opposite: A home economist prepares a turkey for a cooking method test, undated. *Records of the Bureau of Human Nutrition and Home Economics.*

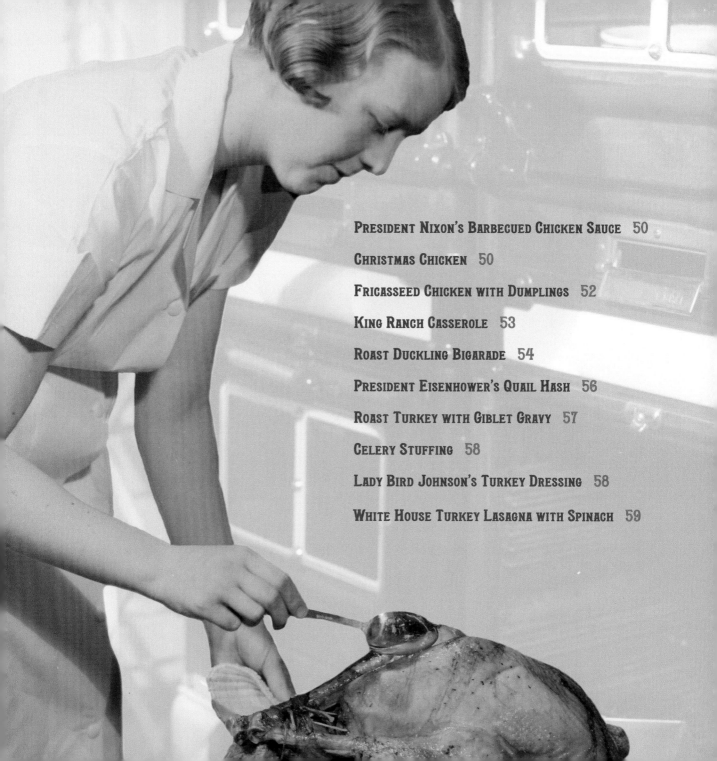

PRESIDENT NIXON'S BARBECUED CHICKEN SAUCE

Two small chickens cut into halves

To ½ cup melted butter, add the following:

Juice of two lemons

1 teaspoon garlic salt

1 tablespoon paprika

1 tablespoon oregano

Salt and pepper to taste

Marinate chicken for three or four hours in sauce.
Barbecue—basting often with remainder of sauce.
Or to bake—oven at 325°F—bake 45 minutes.

Serves 4

Richard Nixon Presidential Library and Museum

Detail of *Pitch in and Help!* poster, 1944. *Records of the Office of Government Reports.*

CHRISTMAS CHICKEN

A plump fowl, weighing 4 to 6 pounds	2 tablespoons chopped onion
4 or 5 medium-sized potatoes	2 tablespoons parsley
1 cup raisins, without seeds	Flour
3 cups canned tomatoes	Butter
	Salt and pepper

Simmer the fowl in a small quantity of salted water until tender. Remove from the broth. Set the fowl aside for stuffing. To the chicken broth add the canned tomatoes and the finely chopped mild onion. Let this sauce cook down. In the meantime, prepare the stuffing by cooking and mashing the potatoes and adding to them the raisins and enough milk to make the mixture the stiffness of ordinary mashed potatoes. Stuff this, while still hot, into the body cavity and neck of the fowl. Crowd in all the stuffing possible. Pour a little melted butter over the chicken. Put it in the oven to brown. Thicken the tomato sauce to the consistency of a gravy and add 2 or 3 tablespoons of finely chopped parsley and green pepper, if desired. When the chicken and the surface of the potato stuffing have become delicately brown, place on a large hot platter. Pour part of the sauce around the chicken and serve at once.

Aunt Sammy's Radio Recipes, Records of the U.S. Department of Agriculture

The "chicken for every pot" phrase is often cited as part of a speech given by Herbert Hoover. However, no evidence has been found that he ever uttered it. This advertisement was created and put forth for publication by Republican businessmen in New York City in 1928. *Herbert Hoover Presidential Library and Museum.*

A Chicken *for* Every Pot

THE Republican Party isn't a *"Poor Man's Party:"* Republican prosperity has erased that degrading phrase from our political vocabulary. The Republican Party is *equality's* party— *opportunity's* party—*democracy's* party, the party of *national* development, not *sectional* interests—the *impartial* servant of every State and condition in the Union.

Under higher tariff and lower taxation, America has stabilized output, employment and dividend rates.

Republican efficiency has filled the workingman's dinner pail — and his gasoline tank *besides* — made telephone, radio and sanitary plumbing *standard* household equipment. And placed the whole nation in the *silk stocking class.*

During eight years of Republican management, we have built more and better homes, erected more skyscrapers, passed more benefactory laws, and more laws to regulate and purify immigration, inaugurated more conservation measures, more measures to standardize and increase production, expand export markets, and reduce industrial and human junk piles, than in any previous quarter century.

Republican prosperity is written on *fuller* wage envelops, written in factory chimney smoke, written on the walls of new construction, written in savings bank books, written in mercantile balances, and written in the peak value of stocks and bonds.

Republican prosperity has reduced hours and *increased* earning capacity, silenced *discontent*, put the proverbial "chicken in every pot." And a car in every backyard, to boot.

It has *raised* living standards and *lowered* living costs.

It has restored financial confidence and enthusiasm, changed *credit* from a *rich* man's privilege to a *common*

utility, *generalized* the use of time-saving devices and released women from the thrall of *domestic drudgery.*

It has provided every county in the country with its concrete road and knitted the highways of the nation into a *unified* traffic system.

Thanks to Republican administration, farmer, dairyman and merchant can make deliveries in *less* time and at *less* expense, can borrow *cheap* money to refund exorbitant mortgages, and stock their pastures, ranges and shelves.

Democratic management *impoverished* and *demoralized the railroads*, led packing plants and tire factories into *receivership*, squandered billions on *impractical* programs.

Democratic maladministration issued *further* billions on mere "scraps of paper," then encouraged foreign debtors to believe that their loans would never be called, and bequeathed to the Republican Party the job of *mopping up the mess.*

Republican administration has *restored* to the railroads solvency, efficiency and par securities.

It has brought rubber trades through panic and chaos, brought down the prices of crude rubber by smashing *monopolistic rings*, put the tanner's books in the *black and* secured from the European powers formal acknowledgment of their obligations.

The Republican Party rests its case on a record of stewardship and performance.

Its Presidential and Congressional candidates stand for election on a platform of sound practice, Federal vigilance, high tariff, Constitutional integrity, the conservation of natural resources, *honest* and *constructive* measures for agricultural relief, sincere enforcement of the laws, and the right of *all* citizens, regardless of *faith* or *origin*, to share the benefits of opportunity and justice.

Wages, dividends, progress and prosperity say,

"Vote *for* Hoover"

Paid for by a member of the Republican Business Men, Inc.

Those wishing to see similar advertisements in other New York papers may send cheques to the Republican Business Men, Inc., 4 West 40th Street

GENERAL COMMITTEE

George Henry Payne, Chairman.

L. F. Loree   wm. H. Vauclain   Wm. H. Hamilton   Julius Rosenwald   Albert I. Gray   Edson S. Lott   F. R. McKnight   Wm. Cooper Procter   R. B. Strassburger
George Whitney   Henry Rogers Winthrop   Frank C. Henson   J. Horace Harding   Geo. W. W. Atterbury   Wm. Ziegler, Jr.   Kermit Roosevelt   Edmond E. Wise   Albert Breech

51

FRICASSEED CHICKEN with DUMPLINGS

Cut chicken into pieces for serving. Roll each piece in flour and brown in hot fat. Browning the chicken before cooking, it helps retain and develop the flavor. After the pieces are browned, simmer until tender in enough water to cover. When it is done, take the chicken out and cook dumplings in the gravy. Serve the chicken in the center of a platter with the dumplings around the edge. Pour the gravy over the chicken.

DUMPLINGS

1 cup flour
2½ teaspoons baking powder
½ teaspoon salt
1 egg
⅓ cup milk

Sift the flour, baking powder, and salt together. Beat the egg well, add the milk, and mix the dry ingredients. Drop by small spoonfuls into the chicken gravy. Cover tightly and cook for 15 minutes. The top must not be removed while the dumplings are cooking. If the steam escapes, the dumplings will not be light.

Aunt Sammy's Radio Recipes, Records of the U.S. Department of Agriculture

President Lyndon B. Johnson and Vice President–Elect Hubert Humphrey on horseback at the LBJ Ranch, 1964. *Lyndon Baines Johnson Presidential Library and Museum.*

POULTRY

KING RANCH CASSEROLE

¼ cup margarine
1 large onion, chopped
1 can Ro-Tel tomatoes
1 can Cream of Chicken soup
1 can Cream of Mushroom soup
1 cup chicken stock
10 corn tortillas
2 cups diced cooked chicken
1 cup grated Longhorn cheese

Preheat oven to 300°F.

In a large saucepan, melt margarine over medium heat, add onion and cook until transparent.

Add tomatoes, soups, and stock. Cook, stirring until thickened.

In a large flat casserole, layer tortillas, chicken and sauce. Top with cheese and bake 30 minutes.

Serves 6

Lyndon Baines Johnson Presidential Library and Museum

ROAST DUCKLING BIGARADE

1 5½ pound dressed duckling
    (with trimmings and giblets)
2 small carrots, peeled
4 cups water
4 navel oranges
1 teaspoon salt
3 tablespoons sugar
2 tablespoons Curaçao
¼ cup wine vinegar
2 tablespoons arrowroot
2 small onions, peeled
Juice of ¼ lemon
1 bouquet garni (the white part
    of 1 leek and 1 stalk of celery
    cut into about 4-inch pieces
    and tied with string)
Pinch of white pepper

Prepare the duck stock in the following manner: chop up the giblets and trimmings, onions and carrots—brown them in the oil in a saucepan. Drain off the oil, add the water, salt, and bouquet garni. Simmer for 1½ hours then strain stock.

Cut the orange part of the orange peel into tiny slivers about 1 inch long. Blanch in boiling water for 15 minutes and dry. Season the inside of

M E N U

Hors d'Oeuvre

Four Treasures of Duck

Fried Giblets

Roast Duck

Mushrooms and Sprouts

Duck Bone Soup

Lotus Seeds Sweet Porridge

Fruits

the duckling, add one-third of the orange peel and truss. Brown duckling in 425°F oven for 20 minutes, then lower the heat to 350°F turning duck on one side for 35 minutes and the other side for 30 minutes. Skim the fat from the bottom of the pan from time to time. If the duckling is not brown, put it to an upright position and roast for 15 minutes more.

To make the sauce: boil sugar and vinegar over a medium flame until it becomes a dark brown syrup. Remove from the heat and pour in one-forth of the prepared stock. Simmer and stir until syrup is dissolved.

Mix the arrowroot with 3 tablespoons of wine—add the remaining stock and the arrowroot mixture to the hot sauce. Stir in the orange peel and simmer for 3–4 minutes. Check the seasoning and keep hot.

Remove the white skin from the oranges, cut them in slices, and set aside.

Place the duck on a heated platter and keep hot. Skim all the fat from the roasting juice—add the remaining wine and boil, reducing to about 3 tablespoons. Strain into the sauce and simmer. Stir in the Curaçao. If the sauce seems too sweet, add a few drops of lemon juice. Garnish platter with orange slices and pour over some of the sauce. Serve the rest in a gravy boat.

Top: Memorandum from Dwight L. Chapin to members of the President's party encouraging them to practice using chopsticks before President Nixon's historic visit to China, 1972. *Bottom*: President and Mrs. Nixon enjoy dinner in Peking, China, with Chinese Prime Minister Zhou Enlai, 1972. *Opposite*: Menu from dinner given during President Nixon's visit to Peking—the first by a U.S. President, 1972. *Richard Nixon Presidential Library and Museum.*

Richard Nixon Presidential Library and Museum

PRESIDENT EISENHOWER'S QUAIL HASH

Quail	Salt and pepper
Good chicken stock	Flour

Put into sauce pan whatever number of quail seem sufficient for the company. Cover well with stock. Cook slowly for 10 to 15 minutes or until meat can be removed from bones easily.

Remove from burner, strip and dice meat, and season to taste. Add more stock if necessary to cover well.

With small amount of additional stock, make gravy with flour (browned or not as you choose) and pour over diced quail.

Cover and simmer 10 minutes longer.

Dwight D. Eisenhower Presidential Library and Museum

President George Bush enjoys Thanksgiving Dinner with troops, 1990. *George Bush Presidential Library and Museum.*

POULTRY

ROAST TURKEY with GIBLET GRAVY

Draw and singe the turkey. Remove the oil sac and all pinfeathers. Cleanse thoroughly and wipe dry. Rub the surface over with butter and a little salt. Stuff with a dressing made as follows:

6 cups finely broken stale bread

2 teaspoons salt

⅔ teaspoon pepper

¼ teaspoon thyme

½ teaspoon ground sage

1 teaspoon baking powder

¼ pound butter or an equal quantity of turkey fat

½ onion, grated, or more, if desired.

4 stalks celery, chopped

½ cup boiling water

Scissors may be used to cut up the stale bread. Cook the celery and onion in the butter 5 minutes. Mix with the bread, baking powder, seasonings, and hot water. Fill the cavity of the turkey. If a moist and fluffy rather than a dry dressing is preferred, use more water. If there is any surplus, it may be cooked in a separate dish, basted with the drippings from the pan, and served with the dinner.

The turkey may be started in a hot oven (400°F) if a double roasting pan is used. If the turkey is young and tender, it will be done in 1½ hours, during the latter part of which the temperature may be slightly reduced. A large, heavy, or old bird will require considerably longer baking. Keep the bottom of the roasting pan well covered with water during roasting, so that the meat will not dry out.

GIBLET GRAVY:

Save the giblets—heart, liver, and gizzard—for gravy. Bake in the pan beside the turkey or put through the meat chopper and simmer in a quart of water while the turkey is baking. Measure the liquid. To thicken it, use 2 tablespoons of flour blended with an equal quantity of turkey fat to each cup of liquid. Stir gradually into the hot liquid. Add salt and pepper according to taste.

Aunt Sammy's Radio Recipes, Records of the U.S. Department of Agriculture

CELERY STUFFING

1 medium onion, chopped

1 stalk celery with leaves, chopped

⅓ cup butter

2 teaspoons poultry seasoning

2 tablespoons chopped parsley

1 teaspoon salt

Pinch white pepper

5 cups diced stale bread

1 cup giblet broth

2 eggs, beaten

Sauté the onions and celery in the butter until tender but not brown.

Combine the seasoning and the bread and mix together with the onion and celery mixture.

Combine giblet broth and eggs. Add to stuffing—mix well.

About 8 servings

Gerald R. Ford Presidential Library

LADY BIRD JOHNSON'S TURKEY DRESSING

Medium-size pan of corn bread

4 slices of toasted bread

1 stalk chopped celery

3 large onions, chopped

6 eggs

¼ cup butter

Salt, pepper, sage

Stock from turkey

Mix together bread and corn bread that has been crumbled with stock from turkey. Be sure to use enough stock so it will not be stiff. Add eggs and remaining ingredients. Bake slowly one hour.

Serves 8

Lyndon Baines Johnson Presidential Library and Museum

In 1947, President Truman encouraged Americans to conserve food and eat less meat, in order to send more food to the struggling Europeans. A part of his plan was for Americans to refrain from eating poultry on Thursdays—a slight problem in November! In order to stick with the plan, the Trumans ate Thanksgiving dinner that year on Wednesday, the menu of which is above. *Harry S. Truman Presidential Library and Museum.*

WHITE HOUSE TURKEY LASAGNA with SPINACH
"One of First Lady Michelle Obama's Favorites"

1 tablespoon olive oil

1 cup chopped yellow onion

4 cloves garlic, minced

1 pound fresh ground turkey

1 (28-ounce) can plum tomatoes, crushed

1 (6-ounce) can tomato paste

Coarse salt and freshly ground pepper

1 tablespoon chopped fresh
flat-leaf parsley

1 tablespoon chopped fresh basil

16 cooked lasagna noodles
(preferably whole wheat)

15 ounces low-fat ricotta or
low-fat cottage cheese

¾ cup freshly grated Parmesan cheese

1 large egg, beaten

2 pounds fresh spinach, washed, but not dried

1 pound low-fat shredded mozzarella cheese

1. Preheat oven to 400°F.
2. Heat olive oil in a large skillet over medium heat. Add onion and cook until translucent. Add garlic and cook for 1 minute more. Add ground turkey and cook for about 10 minutes. Add plum tomatoes, tomato paste, and season with salt and pepper; let simmer until thickened, about 20 minutes. Stir in basil and parsley; set aside.
3. In a medium bowl, combine ricotta, ½ cup Parmesan cheese, and egg; season with salt and pepper and set aside.
4. Place damp spinach in a large skillet over medium heat; cook until wilted. Remove from heat and set aside.
5. Ladle one-quarter of the turkey mixture into a 9-by-13-inch baking dish; spread to cover. Add a pasta sheet, one-third of the mozzarella, one-third of the ricotta mixture, one-third of the spinach mixture and another quarter of the turkey mixture. Repeat process two more times; top with remaining sheet of pasta. Sprinkle remaining ¼ cup Parmesan over top; transfer to oven. Bake until bubbly, 25 to 30 minutes.
6. Let stand about 5 minutes before cutting; serve.

Children from Bancroft Elementary School in Washington, DC, help First Lady Michelle Obama plant the White House Vegetable Garden, April 9, 2009. *Official White House Photo by Samantha Appleton.*

Servings vary depending on portion size

Courtesy of the White House

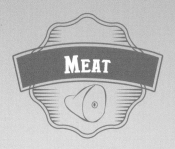

Meat

Sure We'll Share the Meat

There's no "Eating as Usual" anymore—until we win the war.

That's why, among other foods now restricted, we must Share the Meat.

If we share this fine protein food on the government's recommended basis—2½ pounds per week per person over 12 years old—there is enough for all.

After them—You Come First

Ours are the best-fed fighting forces in the world and must be kept so at any sacrifice. Out of the bumper crop of 24 billion pounds of meat this year our fighters and their allies get 6½ billion pounds. This leaves 17½ billion pounds for the rest of us—which is enough… if we plan carefully.

The Good Nutrition of Meat

Stretch your share of meat over the week to insure a regular supply of the fine quality proteins, B vitamins and minerals which meat contains.

Learn more cuts of meat. Serve smaller portions. Plan leftovers carefully. Avoid waste in cooking and at the table. Make every pound count.

Remember, every ounce you go over your share, whether you're eating at home or dining out, takes that amount away from some other American.

If everyone is on the square, everyone will have his share.

Sure We'll Share the Meat poster, 1941–45, *Records of the Office of Government Reports*

This "Pig Cafeteria" was an exhibit created to educate farmers on the science of pig nutrition, undated. *Records of the Office of the Secretary of Agriculture.*

PIG CAFETERIA

BAKED RABBIT

The cleft in the lip of a young and fresh rabbit is narrow, the ears so tender they can easily be torn; claws are smooth and sharp. Old rabbits are the reverse of this.

Remove the head; skin and draw the rabbit; soak it in cold salt water for one hour and longer if necessary, changing the water; wash in fresh cold water; wipe it dry. Make a stuffing of grated bread crumbs, parboil the heart and liver, mince them with a slice of fat pork and a small onion; season the mixture with pepper, salt, and mace, and moisten it with the water in which the heart and liver were boiled, or warm water. Stuff the rabbit with this dressing; sew up the opening closely; lay the rabbit in a baking pan, back uppermost; rub it over with butter or beef-dripping, dredge it with flour, then lay on thin slices of fat pork. Pour into the pan a pint or more of boiling stock or beef-dripping. Put it into the oven and bake with a moderate heat. Baste every few minutes. When the rabbit is browned turn it over in the pan, baste it, dredge it with flour, and continue baking until browned. It should bake in one hour. Serve it in a hot dish with a gravy.

Manual for Army Cooks, 1879, Publications of the U.S. Government

RABBIT in TOMATO SAUCE

1 large rabbit, 2 tablespoons fat
1½ cups tomato pulp and juice, 1 large onion, chopped fine, 2 teaspoons
salt and pepper, 3 cups water

Dip the pieces of rabbit in flour and brown in the fat in a deep iron skillet. Add the chopped onion and tomato juice with the seasonings and the boiling water. Cover and let simmer on top of stove or in the oven for 1 hour. The tomato sauce cooks down and gives a very good flavor to the rabbit. A little more thickening may need to be added just before serving.

Aunt Sammy's Radio Recipes, Records of the U.S. Department of Agriculture

Opposite, background: Ansel Adams photo of sheep flock in Owens Valley, 1941. *Records of the National Park Service.*
Inset: Twenty Sheep to Equip and Clothe Each Soldier poster, ca. 1917–19. Records of the U.S. Food Administration.

CURRY OF LAMB WITH RICE

1. Remove the gristle and fat from a 2 pound lamb shoulder
2. Cut the meat into 1-inch cubes
3. Heat 3 tablespoons of oil and brown the meat with 1 tablespoon of chopped onion
4. Add:
   1 tablespoon of curry powder
   ½ cup chopped celery
   2 tablespoons chopped parsley
   1 tablespoon chopped pimento
   1 tablespoon flour
   (Mix well with meat and vegetables)
5. Add 1½ cups hot water in which 1 teaspoon salt has been added
6. Cover the meat and simmer it for 45 minutes to an hour. Stir frequently
7. Serve with steamed rice

Serves 4

*Gerald R. Ford
Presidential Library
and Museum*

Twenty sheep to equip and clothe each soldier

Boys and girls can help

Join a sheep club

Write to-day for full information to your County Agent or Club Leader or State Director of Extension State Agricultural College

ROASTED RACK OF LAMB WITH PUMPKIN THYME CRUST

2 Frenched racks of lamb

1 cup pumpkin purée

2 teaspoons chopped fresh thyme

1 cup bread crumbs from good bread

3 teaspoons olive oil

Remove excess fat from lamb. Salt and pepper the meat and sear on all sides in a saucepan with a little vegetable oil. Place in a 375°F oven for about 20 minutes depending on the size of the rack. Cook three-fourths of the way from your desired doneness. Let the rack sit on your counter and rest 20–30 minutes. When slightly chilled, spread pumpkin purée on the back and top of the lamb. Mix bread crumbs with salt, pepper, thyme, and olive oil. Roll the rack of lamb in the bread crumbs. Put back in the oven to brown and finish. When done, cut chops and serve.

William J. Clinton Presidential Library and Museum

LBJ RANCH DEER MEAT SAUSAGE

A favorite recipe at the LBJ Ranch is for deer meat sausage. The finished product is recommended for late Sunday morning breakfast with scrambled eggs, hominy grits, hot biscuits, and boiling hot coffee. Or, it can be served for a late-afternoon snack in hot biscuits.

The ingredients are as follows:

½ Deer

½ Hog

25 ounces salt

20 ounces black pepper

8 ounces red pepper

2 ounces sage

Mix together for 200 pounds of sausage.

Lyndon Baines Johnson Presidential Library and Museum

View of deer at sunset on the LBJ Ranch, 1969. *Lyndon Baines Johnson Presidential Library and Museum.*

MEAT

PORTUGUESE BLOOD PUDDING

Another delectable concoction made by the Portuguese of an early generation
is a "blood pudding."

When a hog is killed, the blood is carefully saved. This is mixed into some flour, sugar, and
other ingredients, and [either] steamed, boiled, or baked.

Records of the Work Projects Administration

....

PICKLED PIGS FEET

Place pigs feet in salt pickle for several days. Then boil them for a varying length of time,
depending upon the size of the feet. Take care to remove them from the kettle before the meat
separates from the bones. Split the feet lengthwise, place them in a jar, and cover with vinegar to
which bay leaves, allspice, and whole black pepper have been added.

Aunt Sammy's Radio Recipes, Records of the U.S. Department of Agriculture

....

BAKED BEEF HEAD

Without cooking utensils.

Dig a hole in the ground of sufficient size, and build a fire in it. After the fuel has burned to
coals put in the head, neck downward. Cover it with green grass, earth, and coals. Build a
good fire over the buried head and keep it burning for about six hours.

Unearth the head and remove the skin. A head treated this way at night will be found
cooked in the morning. The head of any animal may be cooked in the same manner.

Manual for Army Cooks, 1879, Publications of the U.S. Government

LIVER DELUXE

1 pound of thin slice beef liver

2 cups brown gravy

Dash of parsley

Dash of salt

1 large onion (sliced thin)

8 pieces of bacon

1 cup of flour

2 tablespoons of butter

Dredge thin slices of liver with flour and brown on each side on a skillet with melted butter. Pour gravy on the liver and season with parsley, salt, and pepper to taste. Simmer for 2 minutes and arrange it on a serving dish. Place bacon on top of liver.

4 servings

Gerald R. Ford Presidential Library and Museum

JAMBALAYA A LA CRÉOLE

1 pound chorices (pork sausage)

1 slice ham

1½ cups rice

1 can tomatoes (small)

2 pods garlic

1 onion (chopped)

2 sprigs parsley, thyme, and bay
   leaf (finely chopped)

Salt, pepper, and cayenne to taste

Wash rice thoroughly. Brown the ham, cut in small pieces, and fry the chorices in a little lard. Drain off the lard which accumulates from frying the meat, leaving only a tablespoonful. Brown onion and other seasonings; add tomatoes. Let cook a few minutes. Pour over the rice and mix thoroughly. Place in a heavy pot, cover, and cook until gravy is absorbed and rice is soft and dry.

The meat may be omitted, and the jambalaya made with shrimp or oysters, the basic recipe being the same.

New Orleans City Guide, 1938, Records of the Work Projects Administration

PAT NIXON'S MEAT LOAF

Start heating oven to 350°F. In a large bowl lightly mix
with fork 1 pound beef and 1 pound pork (ground together)
with ⅓ cup finely chopped onion, 1½ teaspoons seasoned salt,
and ¼ teaspoon ground black pepper. From an 8-ounce can tomato sauce,
add just enough sauce so that meat may be formed into a loaf; place in baking
dish or loaf pan. On top of loaf, lay 3 slices of bacon and pour over it remainder
of tomato sauce. Bake about 1½ hours or until thoroughly done.

Makes 8 servings

Richard Nixon Presidential Library and Museum

SMOTHERED HAM with SWEET POTATOES

1 slice of smoked ham, cut into sizes for serving

3 cups raw, sliced sweet potatoes

1 tablespoon butter or ham drippings

2 tablespoons sugar

1 cup hot water

Brown the ham lightly on both sides and arrange it to cover the
bottom of a baking dish. Spread the sliced sweet potatoes over the
ham. Sprinkle with sugar. Add the hot water and extra fat. Cover the
dish and bake slowly at 350°F (moderate oven) until the ham is tender.
Baste the potatoes occasionally with the gravy. Brown the top well.

*Aunt Sammy's Radio Recipes, Records of the
U.S. Department of Agriculture*

Opposite: Congressman Gerald Ford, his wife, Betty, and their children, Mike, Jack, Susan, and Steve, sit in the
dining room of their home in Alexandria, Virginia, 1958. *Gerald R. Ford Presidential Library and Museum.*

ROSALYNN CARTER'S FLANK STEAK

1½ pounds flank steak
¼ cup soy sauce
¼ cup red or white wine

Combine soy sauce and wine in shallow dish. Marinate flank steak for an hour or longer in mixture, turning occasionally. For medium rare, broil steak 5 minutes on each side, basting once with marinade. Let rest for a couple of minutes before slicing in thin slices across the grain. Always salt steak after it is cooked to avoid toughening.

3 to 4 servings

Jimmy Carter Presidential Library and Museum

TEXAS MEAT MARINADE

½ teaspoon dry mustard
½ teaspoon thyme
½ teaspoon marjoram
½ teaspoon fresh ground pepper
1 teaspoon Yucatan Sunshine habañero pepper sauce

1 tablespoon Worcestershire
2 teaspoons chopped garlic
¼ cup corn oil
¼ cup olive oil
½ teaspoon salt

Mix the dry mustard, thyme, marjoram, and pepper together. Then add garlic, Worcestershire sauce, hot pepper sauce, corn oil, and olive oil. Mix well and pour over your meat of choice covering entire piece of meat with mixture. Marinate for a few hours. Sprinkle with salt just before cooking.

George W. Bush Presidential Library

Opposite: President Eisenhower and former President Hoover grill steaks at Aksel Neilsen's ranch near Fraser, Colorado, on September 1, 1954. *Dwight D. Eisenhower Presidential Library and Museum.*

BARBECUED BEEF

15 pounds beef, ground

½ cup table fat

½ cup lemon juice

1 cup vinegar

2 cups water

2½ quarts catsup

1 cup sugar, brown

¼ cup onion, chopped fine

2 quarts celery, chopped fine

¼ cup mustard, dry

3 tablespoons salt

1. Cook beef in frying or baking pans until done. Stir frequently to prevent lumping. Keep hot.
2. Make sauce by melting fat and combining with liquids, sugar, vegetables, and seasonings.
3. Heat thoroughly but do not cook enough to soften vegetables.
4. Combine sauce with cooked beef and serve on buns.

Yield: 100 ½-cup portions

School Lunch Recipes for 100, 1946, Bureau of Human Nutrition and Home Economics

ROAST VEAL SHOULDER with STUFFING

Remove shoulder bone. Fill cavity with a stuffing made as follows:

2 cups dry bread crumbs

4 tablespoons melted butter

½ teaspoon salt

¼ teaspoon pepper

½ teaspoon onion juice or
finely grated onion

A little sage or thyme, if desired

Mix the seasonings with the dry crumbs and moisten with the butter. Place the prepared meat in the roasting pan. Rub drippings over the surface, sprinkle with pepper and salt, and dredge with flour. The flour forms a crust which holds in the meat juices. Put the meat in a hot oven, in an uncovered roaster, and cook till meat is a good brown color. Then cover the roaster and cook in a slow oven. No basting is required. If there is not enough liquid in the roaster for gravy, wash the tasty crust from the sides of the roaster, add a little water, and make a brown gravy.

Aunt Sammy's Radio Recipes, Records of the U.S. Department of Agriculture

White-faced Herefords on the LBJ Ranch, near Stonewall, Texas, 1968.
Lyndon Baines Johnson Presidential Library and Museum.

President and Mrs.
Reagan walk together at
the Pometta residence in
Geneva, Switzerland, 1985.
*Ronald Reagan Presidential
Library and Museum.*

NANCY REAGAN'S VEAL STEW WITH RED WINE

1. Cut into 12 chunks:
   1½ pounds boneless veal or beef
2. Roll each piece in:
   ½ slice bacon – 6 slices in all
3. Dredge meat lightly with flour
4. Melt in heavy skillet:
   2 tablespoons bacon or other fat
5. Add meat and 12 small peeled onions

Stir ingredients about and permit to
brown on all sides. Remove from pan.
Pour off all but 1 tablespoonful of fat.

6. Stir in 1 tablespoon flour
7. Add and stir until smooth:
   1½ cups consommé or stock
   ½ cup dry red wine

Add veal and onions. Simmer ingredients
closely covered for 1½ to 2 hours
until meat is very tender. Season and
serve with a baked dish.

4 servings

Ronald Reagan Presidential Library and Museum

EAT THE CARP!

The carp discovered America in 1877.

He found the land to his liking. He multiplied and filled the waters with his kind.

He is now big, abundant, useful. He converts useless vegetation and small animals into meat.

This meat is wholesome and nutritious. It contains as much protein as sirloin steak.

It is easily digestible.

It can be cooked in such a way as to remove the muddy taste. It can be boiled, baked, made into croquettes, or fish loaf. Carp jelly, an ancient Swedish dish, is delicious.

There are millions of carp in the United States. The last census shows that 43,000,000 pounds were marketed in one year. Nearly all this came from a few states in the Middle West.

Somebody ate those 43,000,000 pounds of carp.

Therefore the carp must be good to eat.

The carp is good to eat. Carp has not only been eaten, but has been cultivated in Europe for centuries. Europeans know how to cook it.

Catch the carp; buy the carp; cook the carp properly and eat it. Eat the roe; can the roe. Make carp jelly. Can the fish. Smoke it, too.

Eat the Carp! poster, 1911, *Records of the U.S. Fish and Wildlife Service*

Detail of *Save the Products of the Land. Eat More Fish, They Feed Themselves* poster, ca. 1918. *Records of the U.S. Food Administration.*

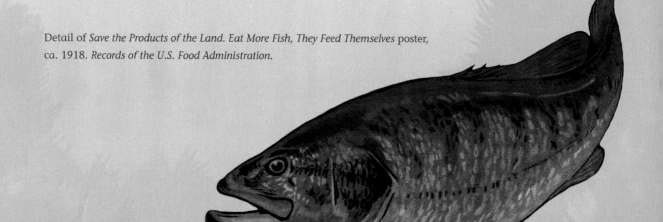

CREAMED OYSTERS

1 quart oysters
2½ cups milk and oyster liquor
½ cup butter
½ cup flour

1 teaspoon salt
⅛ teaspoon pepper
¼ teaspoon onion juice,
   if desired

Cook the oysters in their liquor until the edges begin to curl. Do not let them cook too long or they will be tough. Strain off the liquor. To about 1 cup of this liquor, add enough milk to make 2½ cups. Melt the butter and add the flour, stirring until blended. Add the liquid. Cook for 5 to 10 minutes to do away with the starchy flavor of the flour. Add the oysters and seasoning and serve at once in patty shells or on toast. If creamed oysters stand, the sauce becomes thin.

Editor's note: A "patty shell" is a baked shell made from dough or batter, formed into the shape of a cup to hold food for serving.

Aunt Sammy's Radio Recipes, Records of the U.S. Department of Agriculture

Left: Group of oyster shuckers work in a canning factory in Dunbar, Louisiana, 1911. *Right:* Oyster shuckers at Apalachicola, Florida, 1909. *Records of the Children's Bureau.*

GUMBO

½ dozen hard-shell crabs
1 pound shrimp
2 dozen oysters
1 green pepper
2 stalks celery

1 onion
2 pods garlic
Thyme, bay leaf, and parsley
Salt, black pepper, and
    cayenne to taste

Scald the crabs, clean, and cut in quarters. Make a *roux* by browning a kitchen spoonful of flour in the same amount of hot lard. Add the sliced onion and brown. Put in the crabs and shrimp, cover, and cook about fifteen minutes. Add the other seasonings, chopped, and two quarts of warm water. Cover and cook on a slow fire about two hours. Fifteen minutes before serving, add the oysters and their liquor. Just before serving, turn off the fire and add a tablespoon of filé. Pour into a tureen and serve with boiled rice. Never cook the filé, as it will become very stringy. Okra may be used in place of the filé, but it is cooked with the gumbo. The basic recipe is the same, but chicken, veal, and ham or a combination of veal and a ham bone can be substituted for the crabs and shrimp. After Thanksgiving and Christmas, the leftover turkey may be made into a gumbo with oysters. A deep iron pot is preferable for making gumbo.

Soon-to-be-President Herbert Hoover fishes at Brown's Camp, California, 1928. *Herbert Hoover Presidential Library and Museum.*

Editor's note: Filé, which originated with the Choctaw Nation, is made from dried sassafras leaves pounded to a powder.

New Orleans City Guide, 1983, *Records of the Work Projects Administration*

SALMON with CREAM SAUCE

Heat salmon in can, by placing can in boiling water.

Boil for 20 to 30 minutes. Use a medium white sauce on the fish. Ingredients for the sauce are:

2 tablespoons fat   ¼ teaspoon salt
2 tablespoons flour   Dash of pepper
1 cup milk

Chopped parsley and chopped hard-boiled egg mixed in the sauce make it particularly good.

Aunt Sammy's Radio Recipes, Records of the U.S. Department of Agriculture

FISH PIE

Mashed potatoes, 2 cups   Green pepper, ½
Cooked flaked fish, 2 cups   Salt, ½ teaspoon
Canned tomato, 1¼ cups   Paprika, ½ teaspoon
Fat, 1 tablespoon   Barley flour, 1 tablespoon
Onion, chopped, 2 tablespoons

Melt fat, add onion, and cook until golden brown. Add flour, stir until well blended. Add tomato, cook until thickened; put through a coarse sieve; add to flaked fish and diced green pepper, which has been parboiled. Cover the top with mashed potato, brush with melted fat or milk and cook in a hot oven about 15 minutes, until browned.

Yield: 5 servings

Potato Possibilities, ca. 1917–20, Records of the U.S. Food Administration

Opposite: President Eisenhower shows off his catch, in West Greenwich, Rhode Island, on September 19, 1958. *Dwight D. Eisenhower Presidential Library and Museum.*

FISH

TROUT

In a pan over an open fire, fry some bacon and cook the fish in a combination of the bacon drippings and butter. Before frying the fish, dredge the trout in a sack of corn meal, seasoned with salt and pepper. It takes only about five or ten minutes to cook.

Dwight D. Eisenhower Presidential Library and Museum

PAPRIKOSH

Potatoes, diced, 2 cups

Fish (haddock or other fish),
  ½ pound

Onion, sliced, 2 tablespoons

Parsley, chopped, 2 teaspoons

Fat or olive oil, 2 tablespoons

Salt, ½ teaspoon

Paprika, ½ teaspoon

Water, 1½ cups

Brown onion in fat; add diced potatoes and brown. Add fish, boned and cut into small bits. Mix well together; add parsley, seasonings, and water and cook for about 20 minutes. Serve with a garnish of sliced lemon.

Yield: 5 servings

Potato Possibilities, ca. 1917–20, *Records of the U.S. Food Administration*

POTATO FISH BALLS

Potatoes, 4, medium sized

Codfish, 1¼ cups, shredded

Egg, 1

Salt (if needed), pepper

Fat, 2 teaspoons

Pare and boil the potatoes. Rinse the fish in cold water and press in a fine strainer to remove excess moisture. Cook potatoes until soft; drain, dry, and mash. Add fish, fat, beaten egg, and seasonings. Shape into cakes and fry.

Yield: 12 cakes

Potato Possibilities, ca. 1917–20, *Records of the U.S. Food Administration*

FISH

SALMON LOAF WITH WHITE SAUCE

12 pounds salmon, canned or cooked	¼ cup salt
16 eggs, beaten	1 teaspoon paprika
1¼ gallons bread crumbs, coarse, dry	1 gallon milk and salmon liquid
2 quarts celery, diced	1 quart celery, diced, cooked
½ cup onion, chopped	1 quart green peas, cooked
	1½ gallons white sauce

1. Remove skin and bones from salmon. Drain off liquid and save.
2. Flake salmon and combine with crumbs, celery, onion, and seasonings. If lemon flavor is desired, add ¼ cup grated rind and 1 cup lemon juice.
3. Scald milk and salmon liquid, add to beaten eggs, and combine with first mixture.
4. Fill greased loaf pans two-thirds full and bake at 350°F 45 to 50 minutes.
5. Add cooked celery and peas to white sauce, serve over loaf.

Yield: 100 4-ounce portions

WHITE SAUCE

Table fat, 2 pounds	Salt, 3 tablespoons
Flour, 1 pound	Parsley, chopped fine, ½ cup
Milk, hot, 2 gallons	

1. Melt fat, add flour gradually, blending to a smooth paste.
2. Stir rapidly into hot milk.
3. Cook until thickened, stirring constantly.
4. Remove from heat. Add salt and parsley.

Yield: 2 gallons

School Lunch Recipes for 100, 1946, Bureau of Human Nutrition and Home Economics

Opposite: Johnnie Sauz, a Quinaielt, holding a dog salmon, Taholah, Washington, 1936. *Records of the Veterans Administration.*

SPICY CHEESE GRITS with SHRIMP

2 tablespoons olive oil

1 tablespoon each, finely diced: onion,
   red bell pepper, yellow bell pepper,
   and jalapeño pepper

1 ounce white wine

3½ cups water

¾ cup grits

4 ounces low-fat mozzarella, grated

1–2 cups cooked black beans

16 large shrimp, peeled, cooked, and
   halved (see below)

...for our patrons' health

Keep these cold

*For Our Patrons' Health, Keep These Cold poster,
1944. Records of the Office of Government Reports*

Heat large skillet over medium-high heat, add 1
tablespoon olive oil and stir in 1½ teaspoons garlic. Cook
until light brown, add onion, all the peppers and cook
until onion is transparent. Deglaze pan with wine, add
water and bring to a boil. Stir grits into the boiling water,
turn heat to low and simmer, stirring occasionally for
15 minutes or until done. Stir in mozzarella and season
with salt and pepper. Divide grits among four serving bowls.
Spoon black beans in center and ring with halved shrimp.
Sprinkle with additional mozzarella and diced bell peppers.

SHRIMP

Peel and remove veins from shrimp. Heat skillet over medium heat, add 1 tablespoon
olive oil and ½ teaspoon garlic. Stir until garlic begins to color, add shrimp and sauté until
pink and firm, about 2 minutes. Deglaze pan with 1 ounce of white wine, slice shrimp
lengthwise, and stir into wine mixture.

Serves 4

George W. Bush Presidential Library

FISH

SEAFOOD NEPTUNE

1 teaspoon chopped shallots

1 teaspoon dry mustard

Juice of ½ lemon

1 teaspoon Lea and Perrins sauce

Pinch of white pepper

¼ teaspoon Accent (meat tenderizer)

1 teaspoon chopped parsley

Salt to taste

2 teaspoons chili sauce

1 cup mayonnaise

2 cups diced Lobster meat

1 cup tiny shrimps

2 hard-boiled eggs

1 head Boston lettuce

6 radishes, coarsely chopped

Into 2-quart mixing bowl, put first 7 items. Mix well, then add chili sauce and mayonnaise. Mix well again. Now add lobster meat and shrimps, mix sauce and seafood carefully together.

On round china platter, arrange leaves of Boston lettuce. Mound seafood on platter, decorate with sliced eggs and sprinkle with chopped parsley and chopped radishes.

Serves 6

Richard Nixon Presidential Library and Museum

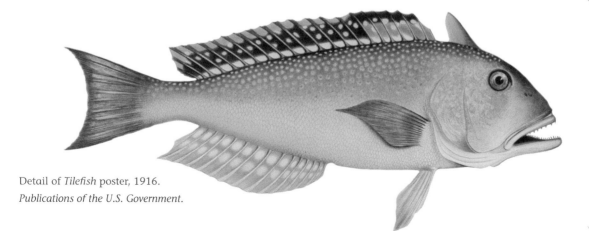

Detail of *Tilefish* poster, 1916.
Publications of the U.S. Government.

LADY BIRD JOHNSON'S SHRIMP SQUASH CASSEROLE

3 cups yellow squash

¾ cup raw shrimp

2 tablespoons margarine

2 tablespoons flour

½ teaspoon salt

⅛ teaspoon pepper

1 cup chicken broth

½ cup whipping cream

1 tablespoon finely minced onion

½ cup coarse bread crumbs

¼ cup grated parmesan cheese

1 tablespoon melted margarine

Wash and dry squash. Cut crosswise into ¼ inch slices.

Thoroughly rinse shrimp under cold water and drain.

Heat 2 tablespoons of margarine in sauce pan. Blend in flour, salt, and pepper. Cook until it bubbles.

Remove from heat and add chicken broth gradually, stirring constantly. Bring to a boil for 1 or 2 minutes.

Blend in cream and minced onions. Mix in raw shrimp.

Layer squash in 1½ quart casserole dish. Spoon half of shrimp sauce over squash. Repeat with remaining squash and shrimp sauce.

Cover tightly and place in a 400°F oven for 30 minutes.

Meanwhile toss crumbs and parmesan cheese with melted margarine.

After 30 minutes, top squash/shrimp with bread crumbs.

Reduce oven heat to 350°F and return casserole to oven for 15 minutes or until crumbs are golden brown.

Lyndon Baines Johnson Presidential Library and Museum

Opposite: Northern Pacific Railway, Takoma, Washington Territory. Shipping first cargo of halibut caught in Puget Sound by crew of schooner *Oscar and Hattier*, 1888. *Records of the U.S. Fish and Wildlife Service.*

JULIE NIXON EISENHOWER'S SPANISH EGGS

1 dozen eggs

12 ounces little shrimp or 2 cans tuna fish

4 large boiled potatoes (peeled)

Mayonnaise with a little lemon juice and salt added

Hardboil eggs, cut in half and take out yolk. Fill eggs with either shrimp or tuna (shrimp better) to which a little mayonnaise has been added. Put all eggs on a platter and cover with a layer of potatoes that have been put through a ricer. Cover this with mayonnaise and then rice the yolks of the eggs over this. Decorate with stuffed olives, sliced, and a few strips of pimento (red).

Very good for brunch or lunch—serve with sliced tomatoes, green salad, or fruit.

Richard Nixon Presidential Library and Museum

SIDES

The potato, as truly as bread, may be called a "Staff of Life." It furnishes fuel for the body. It gives mineral salts which help to keep the blood in good condition. It is easily digested.

It is a good food all the time—but it is an especially good wartime food for Americans, because the use of the potato means the saving of other foods which can be more easily shipped to our own troops and our Allies.

Since all families have potatoes "boiled, baked, mashed and fried," such recipes are not included in this pamphlet. The recipes given here are suggested as more unusual ways of preparation.

Use potatoes extensively!

Potato Possibilities, ca. 1917–20, Records of the U.S. Food Administration

Opposite: Mr. Peanut Goes to War! poster, 1941–45. Records of the War Production Board.

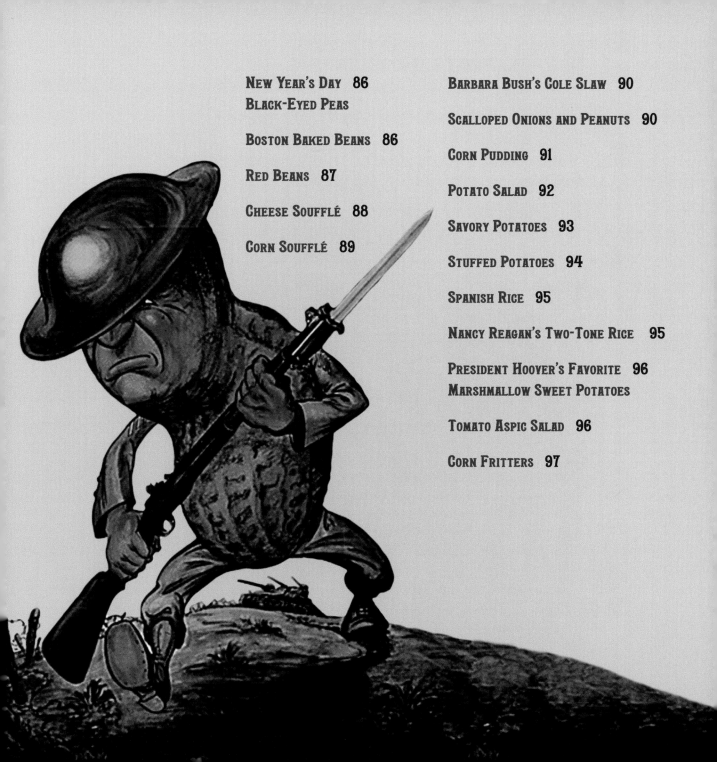

NEW YEAR'S DAY BLACK-EYED PEAS

1 pound fresh black-eyed peas,
  or frozen (if not in season)

2 tablespoons olive oil

2 onions, finely diced

4 garlic cloves, minced

1 bay leaf

6 cups vegetable stock

2 teaspoons fresh parsley, chopped

Salt and pepper to taste

Sweat onions, garlic, and bay leaf in olive oil until fragrant and tender. Add the black-eyed peas and vegetable stock. Simmer until the black-eyed peas are tender, probably 20–30 minutes. Season with salt and pepper. Finish with chopped parsley and serve warm.

Serves 6

George W. Bush Presidential Library

BOSTON BAKED BEANS

6 quarts or 10 pounds navy beans

5 pounds 2 ounces salt pork

6 tablespoons dry mustard

1 pound 12 ounces sugar

1 cup molasses

$\frac{1}{3}$ cup salt

3 gallons soaking water plus fresh

1. Wash beans, cover with water, and soak 12 hours or longer.
2. Cut salt pork into $\frac{1}{3}$-inch cubes; fry until brown.
3. Add other ingredients, except water, to beans and mix well.
4. Put beans into pots, crocks, or deep pans and add water.
5. Cover and bake 7 to 8 hours at 250°F. Uncover and brown the last hour.
6. Add extra hot water during baking, if necessary.

Yield: 100 ½-cup portions

School Lunch Recipes for 100, 1946, Bureau of Human Nutrition and Home Economics

RED BEANS

Red beans are to New Orleans what the white bean is to Boston and the cowpea is to South Carolina.

This is a very nutritious and economical dish and is one of the most popular of all Creole cuisine. Red beans are always served with a dish of boiled rice. Until a few years ago, when New Orleans was not so commercialized, you could purchase a "*quartee* beans, *quartee* rice and a little *lagniappe* to make it nice." *Quartee* means a half a nickel and *lagniappe* was a gift given with a purchase, seasoning of some sort, for instance.

The red beans are soaked in water until the skins shrivel. Pour off the water and put in a deep pot. Cover with water, add chopped parsley, an onion and green onions, a tablespoonful of lard, salt and pepper, a slice of meat, ham, or several strips of bacon. Cook for several hours on a slow fire until thick and creamy.

New Orleans City Guide, 1938, *Records of the Work Projects Administration*

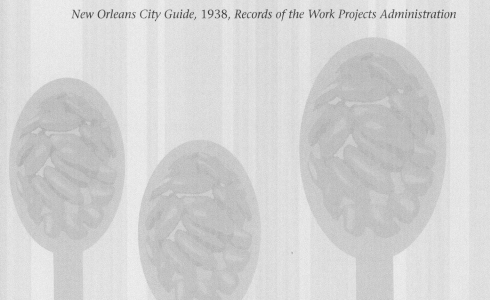

CHEESE SOUFFLÉ

1 pint milk
1¾ cups bread crumbs
3 or 4 eggs
½ pound American cheese
¾ teaspoon salt

Put the bread crumbs and milk together in the double boiler, and heat to the scalding point. Grate the cheese, or shave it into thin, small pieces and stir it into the hot milk and bread crumbs, but do not let it cook. Add the salt. Take this mixture from the heat and while it is cooling, beat the yolks and whites of the eggs separately, and butter a baking dish. The soufflé will cook best in a good-sized earthenware or glass baking dish 3 or more inches deep. After the bread, milk, and cheese mixture has cooled, stir in the beaten egg yolks and fold in the whites. The air beaten into the egg whites makes the soufflé fluffy; therefore mix the egg whites in with careful folding motion. Pour the mixture at once into the buttered baking dish and bake in a very moderate oven for 45 to 50 minutes. Long, slow cooking is one of the secrets of making a perfect soufflé. The moderate heat makes the air bubbles in the egg whites expand until the mixture is light and cooks it thoroughly so that even when a spoon is put into it for serving it does not collapse like a pricked balloon. That is what happens to a soufflé, omelet, or other similar egg dish that has been cooked too rapidly at too high a temperature. Soufflés are not hard to make if one remembers this important point.

Aunt Sammy's Radio Recipes, Records of the U.S. Department of Agriculture

SIDES

CORN SOUFFLÉ
A NIXON FAMILY FAVORITE

3 cans cream-style corn

8 eggs, separated and beaten

3 cubes of melted butter (¾ pound)

1 cup flour (scant)

3 tablespoons sugar

1 teaspoon salt

¼ teaspoon pepper

2 cups half-and-half cream

Combine above and cook until it thickens, then add 3 cans of cream-style corn. Cool to lukewarm. Add 8 beaten egg yolks and 8 beaten egg whites. Pour into a 3-quart buttered Pyrex dish and set in a pan of water to bake. Bake at 350°F for about 1 hour or until knife inserted comes out clean. Pour some melted butter over the top.

Makes 12 servings

Richard Nixon Presidential Library
and Museum

BARBARA BUSH'S COLE SLAW

2 medium heads of cabbage,
   finely shredded (may add
   some purple cabbage for color)

2 medium white or purple
   onions, chopped

4 scallions, finely sliced

2 teaspoons salt

1/3 cup sugar

1 teaspoon dry mustard

1/2 cup cider vinegar

3/4 cup vegetable oil

Freshly ground black pepper
   to taste

4 heaping tablespoons light
   nonfat mayonnaise or
   salad dressing

Sprinkle cabbage with salt and let drain in a colander about 2 hours, squeezing as much water out as possible before continuing. May drain overnight if desired. Add onions. In a small bowl, mix remaining ingredients and stir into cabbage mixture. Adjust seasonings if needed by adding a bit of sugar first and, if necessary, more salt. Cover and refrigerate until ready to serve.

George Bush Presidential Library and Museum

SCALLOPED ONIONS AND PEANUTS

6 medium-sized onions

1/2 cup peanuts, ground

1 cup thin white sauce, made with 1 tablespoon flour,
   1 tablespoon butter, and 1 cup milk

Cook the skinned onions in boiling water until tender. Drain and slice with a sharp knife. Place the onions in layers in a greased baking dish, cover each layer with the cream sauce and the peanuts, and continue until all ingredients are used. Cover the top with buttered crumbs and bake in a moderate oven (350°F) until golden brown. Serve from the baking dish.

Aunt Sammy's Radio Recipes, Records of the U.S. Department of Agriculture

CORN PUDDING

1 16-ounce can whole
   kernel corn, drained
1 16-ounce can cream-
   style corn
3 tablespoons flour
2 tablespoons sugar

Pinch of salt
1 teaspoon baking powder
3 eggs
1 cup scalded milk
2 tablespoons melted butter

Put whole kernel corn into mixing bowl, add flour and mix well. Add cream-style corn, sugar, salt, pepper, baking powder, and melted butter.

Beat eggs in separate bowl, add scalded milk to eggs and beat well again. Pour over corn mixture—mix well—pour into Pyrex dish.

Cook corn pudding in a 350°F oven in "Bain-Marie" (pan with water) on middle shelf for 40 to 45 minutes.

Yield: 1 quart

Gerald R. Ford Presidential Library and Museum

Opposite: Detail of *Mr. Peanut Goes to War!* poster, 1941–45. *Records of the War Production Board. Background:* Display of Corn at the Panama-Pacific Expo, 1915, San Francisco, California. *Records of the Office of the Secretary of Agriculture.*

POTATO SALAD

Potatoes, 3

Onion, 1

Oil, 3 tablespoons

Vinegar, 1 tablespoon

Salt, ¼ teaspoon

DRESSING

Cornstarch, ½ tablespoon

Syrup, 1 tablespoon

Paprika, ¼ teaspoon

Salt, ½ teaspoon

Mustard, 1 teaspoon

Vinegar, ½ cup

Milk, or thin cream, ½ cup

Cook potatoes in skins until tender; peel, dice, and add to mixture of vinegar, oil, onion, and salt. Allow to stand 20 minutes, or longer.

For dressing, mix cornstarch, seasonings, syrup, and vinegar, and cook directly over the fire until boiling. Cook over hot water 20 minutes. Add milk or cream, cook until thickened. Chill. Add to potatoes.

This salad may be varied by the addition of any of the following ingredients:

Hard cooked eggs

Chopped olives

Pickles or pimentos

Nuts

Celery

Smoked fish

Any other salad dressing desired may be used.

Potato Possibilities, ca. 1917–20, *Records of the U.S. Food Administration*

SAVORY POTATOES

Potatoes, 6

Onions, chopped, 2

Fat, 1 tablespoon

Salt, ½ teaspoon

Pepper, ¼ teaspoon

Water, ½ cup

Milk, ½ cup

Cheese, grated, ½ cup

Parsley, chopped,
  1 tablespoon

Pare and slice the potatoes, add chopped onions, parsley, salt, and pepper. Melt the fat in a saucepan; add the potato mixture. Pour in the water, cover tightly and cook gently for 20 minutes. Then add the milk and cook for another 15 minutes. Serve on a hot platter with the grated cheese sprinkled over the top.

Yield: 7 servings

Potato Possibilities, ca. 1917–20, *Records of the U.S. Food Administration*

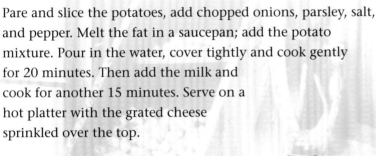

Potatoes move down a conveyer belt before being made into potato flakes, undated. *Records of the Bureau of Plant Industry, Soils, and Agricultural Engineering. Opposite*: Potato display, 1918. *Herbert Hoover Presidential Library and Museum.*

STUFFED POTATOES

Medium-sized potatoes, 3

Salt, ¾ teaspoon

Milk, ¼ cup

Pepper

Bake potatoes until they are tender. Cut into halves; remove the pulp, add seasonings and milk, and beat until smooth. Fill potato shells with the mixture. Brush over with butter or milk; return to oven and bake for 10 minutes.

This dish may be varied by adding to the mashed potato mixture any of the following seasonings before refilling the cases:

½ cup grated cheese

1 pimento put through potato ricer

½ cup chopped meat or fish. Smoked fish is desirable.

The potato case may be partially refilled with mashed potato, and an egg may then be dropped into the center of the case. This should be cooked until the egg is of the desired hardness.

Yield: 6 servings

Potato Possibilities, ca. 1917–20, *Records of the U.S. Food Administration*

SPANISH RICE

3 medium-sized onions

½ cup drippings or butter

½ cup uncooked rice

3 cups fresh or canned tomatoes

3 green peppers cut into strips

2 teaspoons salt

Slice the onions and cook until tender and slightly brown in the melted fat. Remove them from the fat, add the rice, which has been carefully washed and dried, and brown it. Then add the cooked onions, the tomatoes, the green peppers, and the salt. Turn the mixture into a baking dish and bake it until the rice and the peppers are tender.

Aunt Sammy's Radio Recipes, Records of the U.S. Department of Agriculture

NANCY REAGAN'S TWO-TONE RICE

¾ cup each well-washed wild rice and uncooked white rice

3 cups consommé

2 tablespoons each soy and minced onion

Cook wild rice in 1½ cups of the consommé for 10 minutes. Meanwhile, place white rice in a 1 quart baking dish in a slow oven (300˚F) to toast until golden brown. Stir in the remaining 1½ cups consommé, soy, minced onion, and partially cooked wild rice. Bake in a moderate oven (350˚F) for 30 minutes.

Makes 6 servings

Ronald Reagan Presidential Library and Museum

Detail of *Field Marshal "Potato Pete"* poster, undated.
Records of the Office of Government Reports.

PRESIDENT HOOVER'S FAVORITE MARSHMALLOW SWEET POTATOES

6 sweet potatoes

2 tablespoons butter

2 cups chopped walnuts

Nutmeg

Salt

Cream

Marshmallows

Boil the sweet potatoes, mash with a potato masher to remove all strings. Add butter. Add nutmeg and salt to taste (try small amounts the first time!) Add cream enough to make a soft consistency. Fold in walnuts. Put into baking dish and bake for 10 minutes. Cover the top with marshmallows and bake until lightly browned on top.

Herbert Hoover Presidential Library and Museum

TOMATO ASPIC SALAD

2 envelopes gelatin

1 quart canned tomatoes

1 tablespoon finely chopped green pepper

2 tablespoons finely chopped celery

1 tablespoon finely chopped parsley

1 cup very finely shredded cabbage

1½ teaspoons salt

½ teaspoon onion juice

½ teaspoon sugar

Soak the gelatin in a small quantity of water. Boil the tomatoes for 5 minutes and strain through a fine sieve to remove the seeds. Pour the hot tomato juice over the gelatin and stir until it is dissolved. Add the salt, onion juice, and the sugar and chill. When the gelatin mixture is partly set, add the finely shredded vegetables and mix well. Add more salt if needed. Pour into wet custard cups and place in the cold until set. Turn these molds out on crisp lettuce leaves and serve with mayonnaise.

Aunt Sammy's Radio Recipes, Records of the U.S. Department of Agriculture

SIDES

CORN FRITTERS

1 cup liquid, either juice from canned
    corn or milk, or the two mixed

1 cup drained canned corn

1¾ cups sifted cake flour

1 tablespoon melted fat

1 egg

2 teaspoons baking powder

¾ teaspoon salt

Mix the flour, baking powder, and salt. Mix the
juice from the canned corn or milk, or whatever
liquid is used, the egg after it has been beaten
slightly, and the canned corn. Stir this liquid
mixture gradually into the dry ingredients. Add
the melted fat. If the corn is very moist, even
after the liquid has been drained from it, more
flour may be needed.

Fry the corn fritters in deep fat, or if
preferred, in a skillet in shallow fat.
In either case, drop the mixture by
spoonfuls into the fat and fry rather
slowly. The fritters need time to cook through
to the center before the outside becomes too
brown. Drain the fritters on absorbent paper
and serve hot.

*Aunt Sammy's Radio Recipes, Records of the
U.S. Department of Agriculture*

Extra Fancy Cream Sugar Corn label, 1907. *Records of the
Patent and Trademark Office.*

Pure Food Brand

EXTRA FANCY CREAM SUGAR CORN

GUARANTEED
UNDER
THE FOOD AND
DRUGS ACT,
JUNE 30, 1906.
SERIAL No. 1740

THOMAS ROBERTS & CO.
PHILA. PA.
DISTRIBUTORS

SEAL OF PURITY

VEGETABLES

I do not like broccoli, and I haven't liked it since I was a little kid, and my mother made me eat it, and I'm president of the United States and I'm not gonna eat any more broccoli! Now look, this is the last statement I'm going to have on broccoli. There are truckloads of broccoli at this very minute descending on Washington. My family is divided. For the broccoli vote out there: Barbara loves broccoli. She has tried to make me eat it. She eats it all the time herself. So she can go out and meet the caravan of broccoli that's coming in.

President George H.W. Bush news conference, March 23, 1990

Opposite: Get Your Farm in the Fight! poster, detail, 1942. *Records of the Office of Government Reports.*

ASPARAGUS CUSTARD

1 pint milk

2 cups raw asparagus, cut in small pieces

3 eggs

½ teaspoon salt

3 tablespoons butter

Few drops Tabasco

Cook the asparagus in a small amount of water until almost tender. Beat the eggs slightly, add the milk and seasoning, and then the cooked asparagus and the water in which cooked, if not more than half a cup. Grease the casserole, pour in the mixture, and bake in a pan surrounded by water, in a moderate oven, until set in the center. Serve at once.

Aunt Sammy's Radio Recipes, Records of the U.S. Department of Agriculture

Mr. and Mrs. J. E. Bryan are expert canners in their community, 1932. *Records of the Extension Service.*

VEGETABLES

BAKED CUCUMBERS

3 good-sized cucumbers

¾ cup fine dry
   breadcrumbs

3 tablespoons butter

½ teaspoon salt

1½ tablespoons chopped
   onion

1½ teaspoons finely
   chopped parsley

1 tablespoon chopped
   celery

1 cup tomatoes, cut in
   pieces

Wash cucumbers and cut in half lengthwise. Scoop out as much as possible of the pulp without breaking the skin. Brown the onion in the fat, add other ingredients mixed with the cucumber pulp. Stir constantly, and cook five minutes, or until dry. Place the filling in the cucumber shells and bake until the shells are soft and the mixture is brown on top.

Aunt Sammy's Radio Recipes, Records of the U.S. Department of Agriculture

Can All You Can poster, undated. *Records of the War Production Board.*

WILTED DANDELION GREENS

2 quarts dandelion greens
4 tablespoons bacon fat
¼ cup mild vinegar
1 teaspoon salt

Wash the greens thoroughly. Cut finely with scissors. Place the greens in a skillet and add the bacon fat, vinegar, and salt. Cover until the greens are wilted and then serve at once.

Aunt Sammy's Radio Recipes, Records of the U.S. Department of Agriculture

AVOCADO SALAD

Mash 2 medium-size avocados. Stir into slightly thickened lemon Jell-O base made with:

1 package lemon Jell-O
1½ cups hot water
3 tablespoons lemon juice

Stir in 1 can (2½ size) of grapefruit sections drained, and ½ cup chopped celery.

Chill and unmold. Serve with a whipped cream and mayonnaise mixture.

Richard Nixon Presidential Library and Museum

BAKED PUMPKIN and WINTER SQUASH

Cut the pumpkin or squash into slices and remove the seeds. Put it into a broad, shallow baking pan, adding very little water. Put it in the oven and bake with a gentle heat. It requires a long time to bake, and should not only be done, but dry. When baked, season with butter, pepper, and salt. The slices may be pared and put into the baking pan in layers.

Manual for Army Cooks, 1879, Publications of the U.S. Government

MAMIE EISENHOWER'S FLUFFY TURNIPS

6 medium turnips	⅛ teaspoon basil
2 egg yolks	1 teaspoon grated lemon rind
1 teaspoon salt	2 egg whites
Dash of cayenne pepper	2 tablespoons brown sugar

Cook cubed turnips until tender, about 20 minutes. Drain and mash. Beat egg yolks and add to turnips along with salt and pepper, basil, and lemon rind. Beat egg whites and fold gently into turnip mixture. Pour into casserole, sprinkle with brown sugar and bake 20 minutes.

Serves 6

Dwight D. Eisenhower Presidential Library and Museum

Portrait of Mamie Eisenhower, around age 17, 1913.
Dwight D. Eisenhower Presidential Library and Museum.

103

CABBAGE and CARROT SALAD

Use equal parts of grated carrots and finely shredded cabbage. Mix the carrots and cabbage together with salad dressing until well blended. Serve on crisp lettuce.

Aunt Sammy's Radio Recipes, Records of the U.S. Department of Agriculture

SAUERKRAUT

The cabbage must be firm. Trim, pick over, wash, and shred it fine with a very sharp knife. The stalk should not be used. Line the bottom and sides of a barrel, keg, or crock with cabbage leaves and put into it a layer of cabbage three or four inches deep; pound this down well with a wooden pounder, then sprinkle over it a small handful of salt, preferably table salt, then cabbage, then pound, then salt, and so on, until four layers are put in. Cover the cabbage with a board cut to fit loosely on the inside of the barrel. Pound hard on the board until the cabbage is a compact mass. Take off the board and repeat the process as directed, until the barrel is full. Cover it with cabbage leaves, the leaves with a piece of clean cloth, on the cloth lay the board, and on this put a heavy weight to keep the mass of cabbage down. Set it away in a cool, dry place to ferment. As soon as the sauerkraut commences to effervesce, the covering of leaves should be thrown away, the scum removed, the kraut re-covered with a clean cloth, the board and weight thoroughly washed and replaced; and, as perfect cleanliness is necessary for its preservation, this process should be frequently repeated during the winter.

It is ready for use in 20 or 25 days. It may be eaten raw, or boiled with or without pork or bacon.

Manual for Army Cooks, 1879, Publications of the U.S. Government

SUCCOTASH

Succotash is made with green corn and beans, the proportion being two-thirds corn to one-third beans. String beans may be used. Cut the corn from the cob and shell the beans. If string beans are used, string and cut them into half-inch pieces. Put them into a pot of boiling salt water, enough to cover them. Cover and stew gently until tender, stirring frequently. When cooked, drain. To two quarts of succotash add about a half pint of milk, then stir in a piece of butter about the size of an egg, and one or more tablespoonfuls of blended flour. Stir it constantly till it boils up once. Season with pepper and also salt, if necessary.

Succotash may be made of dried beans and dried corn. They must be soaked overnight in hot water.

Manual for Army Cooks, 1879, Publications for the U.S. Government

Opposite: Raised 'em Myself in My U.S. School Garden poster, 1919. Publications of the U.S. Government.

LBJ RANCH PICKLED OKRA

3 pounds whole okra
6 hot peppers
6 cloves peeled garlic
1 quart vinegar
1⅓ cups water
½ cup salt
1 tablespoon mustard seed

Wash okra and pack in clean jars.

Add to each jar 1 hot pepper and 1 clove of garlic.

Bring remaining ingredients to a boil. Cover okra with hot liquid, filling to within ½ inch of jar top. Adjust lids.

Process in boiling water for 10 minutes.

Lyndon Baines Johnson Presidential Library
and Museum

Opposite: Detail of *Grow Your Own, Can Your Own* poster, 1943. *Records of the Office of Government Reports.*

FRUIT

"Go back to simple food, simple clothes, simple pleasures. Pray hard, work hard, sleep hard and play hard. Do it all courageously and cheerfully."
—*The Memoirs of Herbert Hoover, Volume 1, 1951*

"The Canning Season" cartoon, 1917. As administrator of the U.S. Food Administration during World War I, Herbert Hoover worked to convince America that "Food will win the war," leading Americans to refer to conserving food as "Hooverizing." *Herbert Hoover Presidential Library and Museum.*

Banana inspection, Baltimore, Maryland,
ca. 1900. *Records of the Food and Drug Administration.*

APPLE BROWN BETTY

Apples, medium size, 5

Fat, 4 tablespoons

Bread crumbs, 1¼ cups

Hot water, ¼ cup

Lemon juice, 1½ tablespoons

Corn syrup, dark, 5 tablespoons

Salt, ½ teaspoon

Cinnamon, ½ teaspoon

Pare and cut apples into thin slices. Mix breadcrumbs with melted fat. Mix together the hot water, lemon juice, syrup, salt, and cinnamon. Into a greased baking dish, put alternate layers of breadcrumbs and apples, pouring part of liquid over each layer of apples. Bake in a moderate oven about 45 minutes.

Yield: 20 servings

Sweets without Sugar, 1918, Records of the U.S. Food Administration

RHUBARB BETTY

1 quart sweetened rhubarb sauce, or 1½ quarts raw sliced rhubarb, sugar to sweeten

1 quart fine, dry bread crumbs

4 tablespoons melted butter

Cinnamon or nutmeg

Mix the butter with the crumbs. Place the rhubarb and the crumbs in alternate layers in a greased baking dish, and sift the cinnamon or nutmeg over the top. Bake the pudding in a moderate oven. If rhubarb sauce is used, this will require about 15 minutes. If raw rhubarb is used, cover the baking dish at first and bake for 25 minutes or until the rhubarb is tender. Serve the pudding hot with or without hard sauce.

Aunt Sammy's Radio Recipes, Records of the U.S. Department of Agriculture

HARD SAUCE

¼ cup butter

¾ cup powdered sugar

½ teaspoon vanilla

⅛ teaspoon grated nutmeg

Cream together the butter and sugar, add the vanilla and nutmeg. The secret of creamy hard sauce lies in long beating. Chill before serving. For variety substitute brown sugar and flavor with the grated rind of an orange.

Aunt Sammy's Radio Recipes, Records of the U.S. Department of Agriculture

FRUIT

BARBARA BUSH'S RED WHITE AND BLUE COBBLER
1 can blueberry pie filling, 1 can cherry pie filling

Place blueberry pie filling in bottom of 8 x 8-inch glass baking pan. Spread evenly and then place the cherry pie filling on top, smoothing to edges of pan. Place in 400°F oven to heat while preparing topping.

TOPPING
1 cup flour, 1 tablespoon sugar, 1½ teaspoons baking powder,
½ teaspoon salt, 3 tablespoons shortening, ½ cup milk

Mix dry ingredients and shortening until it is like fine crumbs. Stir in milk and drop by spoonfuls onto hot filling. Bake at 400°F for 25–30 minutes or until brown. Serve topped with vanilla ice cream.

Or try this homemade recipe:

BLUEBERRY FILLING
¼ cup sugar, ½ tablespoon cornstarch, ½ teaspoon lemon juice,
2 cups fresh or frozen unsweetened blueberries

Mix sugar and cornstarch in a saucepan and add all other ingredients. Cook until thickened. Put into 8 x 8-inch Pyrex pan and keep hot in a 250°F oven while making cherry filling.

CHERRY FILLING
1 can sour pie cherries, ½ cup + 2 tablespoons sugar,
1½ tablespoons cornstarch, ⅛ teaspoon cinnamon, ⅛ teaspoon almond extract

In a saucepan, mix dry ingredients. Gradually stir in juice from canned cherries and cook until thickened, adding cherries and flavorings at the end. Smooth cherry filling over blueberry mixture. Keep hot while making topping.

Serves 6

George Bush Presidential Library and Museum

BAKED PEACHES

Select large yellow peaches, pare them, and cut them in halves. Place them in a shallow pan, pit side up. Sprinkle lightly with salt, and dot with butter. Broil under a flame, or bake in the oven until the peaches are hot through and lightly browned.

Aunt Sammy's Radio Recipes, Records of the U.S. Department of Agriculture

President Truman and others with a bushel of peaches, 1947. *Harry S. Truman Presidential Library and Museum.*

BLACKBERRY FLUMMERY

2 cups blackberry juice, from canned or cooked blackberries

½ cup sugar, if juice is unsweetened

3 tablespoons farina, or 4 tablespoons cornstarch

¼ teaspoon salt

2 teaspoons lemon juice

Heat the blackberry juice. Mix the sugar and the farina or cornstarch and the salt, and add to the blackberry juice. Cook in a double boiler for 15 or 20 minutes, or until the mixture thickens and the raw starchy taste disappears. Remove from the stove, add the lemon juice, and beat well. Serve the flummery cold with plain or whipped cream.

Aunt Sammy's Radio Recipes, Records of the U.S. Department of Agriculture

CANDLE SALAD

Place a whole slice of canned pineapple on a lettuce leaf. Stick half a banana upright in the center of the pineapple. Top the banana with a red cherry. Garnish with yellow salad dressing to represent tallow running down the sides of a lighted candle.

Aunt Sammy's Radio Recipes, Records of the U.S. Department of Agriculture

Hawaiian girls pack pineapple into cans, 1928.
Records of the Women's Bureau.

FRUIT CUP

3 quarts pineapple, canned, diced
3 quarts pears, canned, diced
2 quarts peaches, canned, sliced
1 quart orange sections*
1½ quarts bananas, sliced
3½ quarts apples, unpeeled, sliced
3 quarts grapefruit sections†
1½ quarts fruit juices

1. Drain fruits, reserving juices. Combine all fruits except grapefruit sections. Chill.
2. Place fruit in serving dishes, add juice to cover.
3. Top with grapefruit sections.

*Eight No. 150 (medium size) oranges yield 1 quart of sections.
†Eight No. 54 (medium size) grapefruit yield 3 quarts of sections.

Yield: 100 ²/₃-cup portions

School Lunch Recipes for 100, 1946, Bureau of Human Nutrition and Home Economics

FRIED APPLES AND BACON

Select about six good tart apples. Peel them. Cut them in 1-inch cubes. Fry the bacon in a skillet. As soon as the slices of bacon are crisp, remove and drain them on clean brown paper and keep in a warm place. Leave about ¼ cup bacon fat in the skillet and fill it with apples. Sprinkle on 3 tablespoons of sugar. Apples fried this way require a little more sugar than ordinary fried apples. Cover the apples. Cook slowly until tender. Then remove the cover and turn apples gently, so the pieces will keep their shape. Let them brown lightly. They are then almost transparent. Place them on a hot platter, and surround them with the crisp bacon.

Aunt Sammy's Radio Recipes, Records of the U.S. Department of Agriculture

....

JELLIED APPLES

Granulated gelatin, 1¾ tablespoons	Lemon, 1 slice
Cold water, ½ cup	Cooking apples, pared and
Corn syrup, light, 1 cup	quartered, 1 quart
Ginger, ¼ teaspoon	Hot water
Cinnamon, ½ teaspoon	Lemon juice, 1⅓ tablespoons
Cold water, 1½ cups	Lemon rind, ¼ teaspoon

Soak the gelatin in ½ cup cold water for 10 minutes. Cook together the syrup, spices, and slices of lemon, and 1½ cups cold water for 10 minutes. Then add apples, a few at a time, letting them cook until tender, but not broken. Remove from syrup when done and place in a shallow dish. When all apples are cooked, add the syrup to the soaked gelatin; add enough hot water to make 2 cups of liquid; add lemon juice and grated lemon rind; strain; pour over apples and chill.

Yield: 8 servings

Sweets without Sugar, 1918, Records of the U.S. Food Administration

SCALLOPED APPLES

Pare, core, and slice tart apples, preferably those of a kind that will hold their shape when cooked. Place a layer of the sliced apples in a baking dish, sprinkle with sugar, dot with butter, or pour on a little melted butter. Put in another layer of apples and keep on until the dish is heaping full. Press the apples down and put in as many as possible. Cover the dish and cook slowly for 1 to 1½ hours in a 300°F (slow) oven. Fifteen minutes before the apples are to be served, remove the cover and spread buttered breadcrumbs over the top. Return to the oven and let the crumbs become golden brown and crisp. The apples themselves will be in whole pieces and almost transparent. Some kinds will be pink in color. Scalloped apples are good served hot with main course of dinner or supper.

Aunt Sammy's Radio Recipes, Records of the U.S. Department of Agriculture

SWEET PICKLED APPLES

Sweet apples, 8 pounds (26 medium-sized)	Corn syrup, dark, 2 quarts
Vinegar, 1½ quarts	Cinnamon, 4 sticks
Water, 1½ quarts	Whole allspice, 2 tablespoons
Salt, ½ teaspoon	Ginger, if desired
	Whole cloves, 4 tablespoons

Cook together the vinegar, water, salt, syrup, and spices (except cloves) for 5 minutes. Peel and quarter the apples. Stick 2 cloves into each quarter. Drop the apples into the boiling syrup and simmer until tender. Pack in hot jars. Cover with boiling syrup. Partially seal and sterilize for 10 minutes. Seal tightly. Let cool. Label and store.

Sweet pickled pears can be made by substituting pears for apples in the above recipe.

Aunt Sammy's Radio Recipes, Records of the U.S. Department of Agriculture

FRUIT

116

LADY BIRD JOHNSON'S MOLDED CRANBERRY SALAD

1 envelope unflavored gelatin

1¼ cups cold water

1 cup sugar

½ cup chopped celery

½ cup chopped nuts

½ teaspoon salt

2 cups cranberries

Cook cranberries in 1 cup of water for 20 minutes. Stir in sugar and cook 5 minutes longer.

Soften gelatin in ¼ cup cold water; add to hot cranberries and stir until dissolved. Set aside to cool.

When mixture begins to thicken, add chopped celery, nuts, and salt. Turn into mold that has been rinsed with cold water. Chill in refrigerator until firm.

Unmold on serving plate. Garnish with salad greens if desired.

Makes about 6 servings

Lyndon Baines Johnson Presidential Library and Museum

A typical fruit and vegetable stand in Center Market, Washington, DC, 1915. *Records of the Bureau of Agricultural Economics. Background: Theodore Roosevelt replants a Bahai orange tree, 1903. Records of the Bureau of Plant Industry, Soils, and Agricultural Engineering.*

BESS TRUMAN'S BING CHERRY MOULD

1 large can bing cherries

2 packages cream cheese

1 package cherry Jell-O (or any red gelatin)

1 package lime Jell-O

Measure the juice from the cherries and add water to make two cups. Heat and dissolve cherry Jell-O in this. When partly set, add cherries.

Make lime Jell-O with water. When partly set, beat in cheese. Put cheese Jell-O in bottom of mould; let set; then put cherry mixture on top. Serve with mayonnaise.

Harry S. Truman Presidential Library and Museum

SUNBONNET SUE

5 halves of cooked or canned pears or peaches

10 whole cloves

10 almonds

5 thin slices of pimiento

5 tablespoons salad dressing

5 leaves curly lettuce

Arrange the halves of the fruit round side up on the lettuce leaves. The leaf curls up around the fruit and forms the sunbonnet. Place the cloves in the fruit for the eyes, the blanched almonds for the ears, and slip thin slices of canned pimiento into cuts made for nose and mouth. The expressions may be varied. Put salad dressing around the outside of the fruit, to represent golden locks, and arrange a bow of red pimiento under the chin of Sunbonnet Sue.

Aunt Sammy's Radio Recipes, Records of the U.S. Department of Agriculture

NANCY REAGAN'S SWEET AND SOUR DRESSING FOR FRUIT SALAD

½ cup sugar

2 level tablespoons flour

1 teaspoon paprika

½ cup vinegar

½ teaspoon grated onion

1 teaspoon salt

¾ cup oil

1 teaspoon celery seed (soak
   in tablespoon water)

Mix sugar, flour, and paprika; stir in
vinegar; heat until thick in double boiler.
Add onion and salt; cool. Add oil a little at
a time, while beating with a rotary beater.
Add drained celery seed.

Ronald Reagan Presidential Library and Museum

*Harvest War Crops poster, 1945. Records of
the Office of Government Reports.*

Why Save Sugar?

The new sugar crops are short. 50,000,000 pounds of sugar have been lost through submarine sinkings. Germans have destroyed sugar-beet fields and factories in France. Our allies have far less sugar than we and we have not our usual supplies on hand. Our ships are needed for carrying troops and supplies and cannot bring sugar from far distant countries.

Why Do We Eat Sugar?

Mostly because we enjoy its sweetness. It is good food but it is not better for us than bread or potatoes.

How Much Sugar May We Eat?

Our present share is two pounds apiece per month, or six level teaspoons per day. This means all we use in cooked food, tea, coffee, sweet summer drinks, ice cream, and candy.

How Can We Have Sweet Food Without Sugar?

Use sweet substitutes, as molasses, corn syrup, maple syrup, glucose, maple sugar, corn sugar, honey, raisins, dates, or figs.

How Are Substitutes to be Used?

The following recipes will show how to have cookies, cakes, desserts, and even conserves without any sugar at all. Try them and see what good food can be made without sugar.

Sweets without Sugar, 1918, Records of the U.S. Food Administration

Opposite: President John F. Kennedy aboard the *Honey Fitz*, off Hyannisport, Massachusetts, 1963. *John F. Kennedy Presidential Library and Museum.*

DAVID EISENHOWER'S CHOCOLATE BIRTHDAY CAKE

2 ounces bitter chocolate

5 tablespoons boiling water

1½ cups sugar

½ cup butter

4 egg yolks

1¾ cups cake flour

3 teaspoons baking powder

¼ teaspoon salt

½ cup milk

1 teaspoon vanilla

4 egg whites

Melt chocolate over hot water. Add 5 tablespoons boiling water. Cool this mixture slightly.

Sift 1½ cups sugar. Beat butter until soft and gradually add sugar. Blend this mixture until light and creamy.

Beat in egg yolks, one at a time. Add the chocolate mixture.

Sift cake flour twice with baking powder and salt. Add this mixture in 3 parts to the butter mixture. Add milk and vanilla.

Slowly beat batter until smooth.

Beat egg whites until stiff and fold them into cake batter.

Bake cake in two greased 9-inch cake pans in a 350°F oven for about 30 minutes.

Richard Nixon Presidential Library and Museum

A birthday party for David Eisenhower, grandson of President Dwight Eisenhower; in attendance were cowboy movie and television stars Roy Rogers and Dale Evans, 1956. *Dwight D. Eisenhower Presidential Library and Museum.*

SWEETS

CHOCOLATE ICING

2 ounces bitter chocolate

2 cups sugar

1 cup water

2 egg whites

⅛ teaspoon salt

⅛ teaspoon cream of tartar

1 teaspoon vanilla

Boil sugar and water until the syrup forms a soft ball when dropped in cold water. Whip egg whites, salt, and cream of tartar until frothy. Add syrup in a thin stream, whipping constantly. Add vanilla and melted chocolate. Ice cake immediately.

Richard Nixon Presidential Library and Museum

DEVIL'S FOOD CAKE

Corn syrup, ½ cup

Honey, ½ cup

Chocolate, 2 squares

Fat, ¼ cup

Egg, 1

Salt, ½ teaspoon

Wheat flour, 1 cup

Barley flour, ⅔ cup

Soda, ½ teaspoon

Baking powder, 1 teaspoon

Milk, ½ cup

Heat together the honey, syrup, and chocolate, until the chocolate is melted. Add fat, and stir until blended. Add egg, well beaten. Sift together the dry ingredients. Add alternately with milk to first mixture. Stir well. Bake in well-greased layer cake pans in a moderate oven for about 30 minutes.

Yield: 2 layers

Sweets without Sugar, 1918, Records of the U.S. Food Administration

FRUIT CAKE

1 pound raisins	½ cup tart jelly
1 pound currants	½ cup sour cream
¼ pound citron	½ teaspoon soda
½ pound butter	½ teaspoon salt
1 cup chopped nuts	1 cup molasses
4 cups flour	5 eggs
1 cup sugar	1 tablespoon cinnamon
½ cup cider	½ teaspoon nutmeg

Prepare all the fruit before mixing it. Cut the citron into very small pieces. Cream the butter and sugar. Separate the eggs, and add the yolks after the butter and sugar are blended. Add the liquids—cider, jelly, sour cream, and molasses. Mix the salt, soda, and spices with one-half the flour. Mix the other half of the flour with the fruit and nuts. Add the dry ingredients gradually to the liquid ingredients, then the floured fruit, and last the whites of the eggs. If the fruit is well covered with flour, it will be scattered throughout the cake, and will not settle to the bottom.

Bake the cake in a tube pan lined with greased paper in a slow oven (275°F to 300°F). A low fire allows the heat to penetrate the cake mixture slowly and does not dry it out or burn the crust.

If the recipe for this fruit cake is doubled, it should be baked in two pans. It is better to bake fruit cakes in medium-sized loaves rather than in large loaves.

Aunt Sammy's Radio Recipes, Records of the
U.S. Department of Agriculture

SWEETS

INEXPENSIVE CHRISTMAS CAKE

½ pound salt pork (chopped fine)   1½ cups boiling water

1½ cups molasses   ½ teaspoon nutmeg

1 cup sugar (brown)   1 teaspoon cinnamon

1½ teaspoons soda   1 teaspoon baking powder

1 pound raisins (cut)   4½ cups flour

Measure molasses in bowl and add soda. Let it become foam; add raisins, spices, pork, and sugar, lastly flour, which has been sifted with the baking powder. Bake in bread pans in moderate oven.

More fruit, like candied citron, lemon, and orange peel, can be added.

Franklin D. Roosevelt Presidential Library and Museum

TRUMAN FAMILY POUND CAKE

One pound of white sugar   One pound of butter

One pound of flour   One teaspoon lemon

Nine good size eggs   extract

Beat the egg yolks and blend in all other ingredients except the egg whites which are beaten until stiff and folded in last. Bake in a very slow oven about two hours. Should be baked in a pan with a flue in the center. Ice the cake with white icing and decorate with walnut meat halves.

Harry S. Truman Presidential Library and Museum

President Truman blows out the candles on this United Nations cake made from the Truman Family Pound Cake recipe, 1951. *Harry S. Truman Presidential Library and Museum.*

THE WEDDING CAKE OF PATRICIA NIXON AND EDWARD FINCH COX

Heat oven to 325°F. Use 12 x 2-inch round, brown paper–lined cake pan with a 3-inch collar.

1. Cream together in blender:
   1 pound sugar (2¼ cups)
   1 pound butter, room temperature
   8 ounces cake flour (2 cups plus 1 tablespoon)
   Grated rind of 2 lemons
   Pinch of salt
2. Add slowly 11 egg whites, unbeaten
3. Sift together:
   1 pound cake flour (4 cups and 2 tablespoons)
   ⅛ ounce baking powder (2½ teaspoons)
   Then add to Step #2 mixture slowly until smooth.
4. Beat: 7 egg whites
   7 ounces sugar (1 cup)
   Add sugar slowly to egg whites before egg whites are completely stiff.
5. Fold egg whites into Step #3 mixture.
6. Pour batter into pan and bake for about 60–70 minutes.

Patricia Nixon and Edward Finch Cox cutting their wedding cake, June 12, 1971. *Richard Nixon Presidential Library and Museum.*

Richard Nixon Presidential Library and Museum

UPSIDE-DOWN PINEAPPLE CAKE

PINEAPPLE MIXTURE

½ cup sugar

2 tablespoons butter

2 tablespoons pineapple juice

3 slices pineapple

Stir the sugar in a smooth frying pan until it is melted, then allow it to brown. Add the butter and the pineapple juice and cook until a fairly thick sirup [sic] is formed. Place the sections of pineapple in the sirup and cook for 1 or 2 minutes or until they are light brown, turning them occasionally. Have ready a well-greased heavy baking pan or a baking dish, place the pineapple on the bottom, and pour the sirup over it. Allow this to cool so it will form a semisolid surface, then pour in the following cake batter.

CAKE BATTER

¼ cup butter

½ cup sugar

1 egg

½ cup milk

1½ cups soft wheat flour

2 teaspoons baking powder

⅛ teaspoon salt

1 teaspoon vanilla

Cream the butter, add the sugar, the well-beaten egg, and vanilla. Sift the dry ingredients together twice and add alternately with the milk to the butter, sugar, and egg mixture. Pour this over the pineapple. The batter is rather thick and may need to be smoothed on top with a knife. Bake slowly in a very moderate oven (300°F to 325°F) for 45 minutes. Loosen the sides of the cake, turn it out carefully, upside down. If the fruit sticks to the pan, lift it out and place it on the cake in the place where it should be. Serve with or without whipped cream or hard sauce (see page 110).

Aunt Sammy's Radio Recipes, Records of the U.S. Department of Agriculture

WAR TIME STRAWBERRY SHORTCAKE

Cornmeal, ¾ cup

Barley flour, 1¼ cups

Baking powder, 3 teaspoons

Salt, 1 teaspoon

Sugar, 3 tablespoons

Fat, 3 tablespoons

Egg, 1

Milk, ⅓ cup

Sift together the dry ingredients; cut in the fat. Beat egg; add milk. Add liquids to dry ingredients. Roll to ½ inch thickness on floured board. Cut into shapes. Bake in a hot oven about 14 minutes.

To 3 cups strawberries, add sugar to sweeten. Crush slightly. Break open the shortcake. Spread with butter; fill center with sweetened berries. Cover top with berries.

Yield: 7 shortcakes (generous servings)

Without Wheat, 1918, Records of the U.S. Food Administration

CREAM PUFFS

½ cup butter

1 cup hot water

1 cup flour

4 eggs

¼ teaspoon salt

Add the flour to the hot water and bring to the boiling point, and add the flour and salt, all at one time. Stir rapidly and constantly until the paste leaves the sides of the pan. Remove from the fire and when cool add the eggs one at a time, beating until thoroughly blended with the paste mixture. Drop by spoonfuls on a greased baking sheet about 2 inches apart. During baking the dough expands to twice or more its original size. Bake in a hot oven 450°F to 475°F until puffed and a golden brown. When cool, cut and fill the lower half with seasoned whipped cream, crushed fruit, or custard mixture. Cover with the other half of the puff and sprinkle powdered sugar over the top.

Makes 8 medium-sized puffs

Aunt Sammy's Radio Recipes, Records of the U.S. Department of Agriculture

SWEETS

DEEP DISH APPLE PIE

6 tart apples	Grated rind of 1 lemon
½ cup sugar	Grated rind of 1 orange
½ cup brown sugar	3 tablespoons butter or margarine
½ teaspoon nutmeg	½ pastry recipe (below)

Pare and core apples; cut into eights. Place in deep, greased baking dish. Combine sugar, brown sugar, nutmeg, lemon rind, and orange rind. Sprinkle over apples. Dot with butter or margarine. Top with thin sheet of pastry, pricked in a design. Bake in hot oven (425°F).

PASTRY

2 cups flour

¾ teaspoon salt

⅔ cup shortening

Cold water

Sift flour; measure. Mix and sift flour and salt. Cut in shortening with 2 knives or pastry blender until flour shortening particles are about the size of small peas. Sprinkle 1 tablespoon cold water over mixture and mix in lightly with a fork. Continue adding water in this fashion until pastry gathers around fork in a soft ball. Divide pastry in half and roll each half separately on lightly floured board to ⅛-inch thickness. Handle rolling pin very lightly. Makes enough for two-crust 9-inch pie.

Make half this recipe for deep dish or one-crust pies.

Dwight D. Eisenhower Presidential Library and Museum

President and Mrs. Eisenhower pose for their portrait on the occasion of their 39th wedding anniversary in Gettysburg, Pennsylvania, 1955. *Dwight D. Eisenhower Presidential Library and Museum.*

PRESIDENT'S PECAN PIE (NEW YEAR'S EVE FAMILY FAVORITE)

1 cup sugar

½ stick butter (unsalted and melted)

1 teaspoon salt

1 teaspoon vanilla extract

1 cup plus 3 tablespoons dark corn syrup

4 large eggs, beaten

1–2 cups pecan halves

10-inch pie crust (recipe below)

Combine sugar, butter, salt, and vanilla, and mix together. Add corn syrup and blend until just combined. Add eggs and blend till mixture is smooth. Place pecan halves on the bottom of the pie crust. Pour filling over the pecans. (Pecans will float to the top.) Bake at 325°F until filling is set, about 55–75 minutes. Let cool. Serve warm with vanilla ice cream or whipped cream.

Makes one pie

PIE CRUST

1 cup plus 2 tablespoons all-purpose flour

½ cup cake flour

3 teaspoons sugar

⅓ cup shortening

¾ stick butter (unsalted, cold, and diced)

1 teaspoon salt

3-4 tablespoons very cold water

Combine both flours, salt, and sugar, and sift into a bowl. Using a fork or pastry cutter, cut butter and shortening into the dry ingredients until pea-sized pebbles form. Add water to mixture. Work just until a dough is formed. Form a ball, wrap with plastic, and refrigerate for 2 hours. Divide into two balls. On a lightly floured surface, roll out each dough ball into a circle. Line a 9- or 10-inch pan with the dough. Crimp edges and chill until ready to use.

Makes 2 crusts

George W. Bush Presidential Library

Background: Pie contest with Dr. Louise Stanley, first head of the Department of Home Economics, judging pies with Mary Lindsay, ca. 1920. *Records of the Bureau of Human Nutrition and Home Economics.*

PUMPKIN PECAN PIE

4 slightly beaten eggs
2 cups canned or mashed
   cooked pumpkin
1 cup sugar

½ cup dark corn syrup
¼ teaspoon salt
1 teaspoon vanilla
½ teaspoon cinnamon

1 unbaked 9-inch pie shell
1 cup chopped pecans

Combine the ingredients except pecans. Pour into pie shell. Top with pecans.
Bake at 350°F for 40 minutes, or until set.

Ronald Reagan Presidential Library and Museum

SOUR CREAM COOKIES

½ pound butter or margarine
1 cup granulated sugar
1 cup brown sugar
3 eggs

1 teaspoon salt
1 teaspoon vanilla
1 cup sour cream
3 cups flour

1 teaspoon baking soda
1 teaspoon baking powder

Combine butter or margarine with sugars and slightly beaten eggs. Beat about 2 minutes at medium speed.
Add vanilla. In a separate bowl, combine dry ingredients. Add to other ingredients and beat another
minute. Drop by heaping teaspoonfuls onto an ungreased cookie sheet. Bake at 375°F for 8 to 10 minutes or
until light brown. If you want, you can cool cookies completely, then spread with creamy vanilla frosting.

Herbert Hoover Presidential Library and Museum

CORN FLAKE MACAROONS

Egg whites, 2
Corn syrup, ½ cup
Salt, ⅓ teaspoon

Corn flakes, 2 cups
Coconut, 1 cup

Beat egg whites until stiff. Fold in syrup, salt, corn flakes, and coconut. Drop mixture from
tip of teaspoon on well-greased tin, about 1 inch apart. Bake in a moderate oven about 10
minutes until delicately brown. Remove from pan while warm.

Yield: 24 macaroons

Sweets without Sugar, 1918, Records of the U.S. Food Administration

PEANUT BRITTLE

3 cups granulated sugar	2 tablespoons soda
1½ cups water	½ stick butter
1 cup white corn syrup	1 teaspoon vanilla
3 cups raw peanuts	

Boil sugar, water, and syrup until spins thread; add peanuts. After adding peanuts, stir continually until syrup turns golden brown. Remove from heat; add remaining ingredients; stir until butter melts. Pour quickly on 2 cookie sheets with sides. As mixture begins to harden around edges, pull until thin.

Jimmy Carter Presidential Library and Museum

PRALINE ICE CREAM BOMBE

1 quart vanilla ice cream
½ pint whipping cream
4 ounces praline paste
4 ounces ground toasted hazelnuts
2 teaspoons melted sweet chocolate

Soften vanilla ice cream. Whip cream and 2 teaspoons sweet chocolate. Fold whipped cream, toasted hazelnuts and praline paste into ice cream. Fill in forms and freeze over night. Unmold and decorate with whipped cream and hazelnut chocolate candy (ground toasted hazelnuts in sweet chocolate).

8+ servings

Gerald R. Ford Presidential Library and Museum

DINNER

Sterling Chenin Blanc 1972

New England Lobster en Bell
Sauce Rémoulade

Beaulieu Vineyard Cabernet Sauvignon 1968

Saddle of Veal
Rice Croquettes
Broccoli Mornay

Garden Salad
Trappist Cheese

Schramsberg Blanc de Blancs 1973

Peach Ice Cream Bombe
with Fresh Raspberries
Petits Fours

Demitasse

THE WHITE HOUSE
Wednesday, July 7, 1976

SWEETS

PERSIMMON PUDDING with BRANDY WHIPPED CREAM SAUCE

½ cup melted butter

¼ teaspoon salt

1 cup persimmon pulp
(3–4 very ripe)

3 tablespoon brandy

1 cup seedless raisins

1 cup sugar

1 teaspoon ground cinnamon

2 teaspoons baking soda

1 teaspoon vanilla

1 cup flour, sifted

¼ teaspoon nutmeg

2 teaspoons warm water

2 eggs, slightly beaten

Chopped nuts (optional)

Stir together melted butter and sugar. Resift flour with salt, cinnamon, and nutmeg, and add to butter and sugar mixture. Add persimmon pulp, soda dissolved in warm water, brandy, and vanilla. Add eggs, mixing thoroughly, but lightly. Add raisins and nuts, stirring until mixed. Put in buttered steam-type covered mold and steam 2½ hours. Flame at table with brandy.

BRANDY WHIPPED CREAM SAUCE

1 egg

Dash of salt

⅓ cup melted butter

1 tablespoon brandy flavoring

1 cup sifted powdered sugar

1 cup whipping cream

Beat egg until light and fluffy. Beat in butter, powdered sugar, salt, and brandy flavoring. Beat whipping cream until stiff. Gently fold into first mixture. Cover and chill until ready to serve. Stir before spooning on pudding.

Ronald Reagan Presidential Library and Museum

Opposite Top: President Ford and Queen Elizabeth dance during the State Dinner in honor of the Queen and Prince Philip at the White House, July 7, 1976. *Opposite Bottom:* Menu for State Dinner in honor of the Queen and Prince Philip at the White House, July 7, 1976. *Gerald R. Ford Presidential Library and Museum.*

FONDANT

2 cups granulated sugar

¾ cup boiling water

⅛ teaspoon cream of tartar

Put the sugar, water, and cream of tartar into a saucepan over a hot fire. Stir constantly until, but not after, the sugar has dissolved. Do not splash the sirup [sic]. Remove the spoon and do not use it again after the sirup boils. Remove the sugar grains or the crystals with a dampened brush or a clean wet cloth. Cover the pan for a few minutes. Let the sirup boil until it reaches a temperature of 235°F or until it forms a soft ball when dropped in cold water. Be sure the bulb of the thermometer is covered and does not touch the bottom of the pan. Pour the sirup in a thin sheet onto a chilled platter so it will cool quickly. Do not scrape out the saucepan. When the sirup is cool, work it until it creams with a flat wooden spoon. When it forms a soft solid ball, work it with the palms of the hands in the same way as bread dough until it is smooth.

Sugar: Save it poster, ca. 1917–19.
Records of the U.S. Food Administration.

Place the fondant in an earthenware or glass dish. Wet a clean cloth in hot water, wring out well, and lay over the top of the candy. After about 24 hours the fondant is ready to mold. Fondant made in this way will keep for months in a cold place if covered with a moist cloth or stored in a tightly covered jar.

The following are a few ways in which fondant may be used:
Form the fondant into small balls with the palms of the hands and press halves of walnut, pecan, or other nut kernels into them; or roll the balls into finely chopped nuts or shredded coconut or work these into the fondant before forming it into balls. Irregular shaped balls of fondant may be rolled in cinnamon for "cinnamon potatoes." Gouge out "eyes" to make them more realistic. Candied fruits, such as cherries, pineapple, cranberries, grapefruit peel, and citron may be used in the center of fondant balls or pressed into the surface.

SWEETS

With or without added nut meats, fondant may be used to stuff dates or prunes.

Fondant may be melted and used to cover various kinds of fruits such as strawberries and white grapes. Firm fruits with unbroken skins should be used for this purpose, and a little of the stem should be left on them. They should be dipped very quickly into the melted fondant.

Fondant may also be melted, flavored with oil of peppermint, oil of wintergreen, oil of roses, vanilla, or almond extract, and dropped from a teaspoon onto waxed paper to make wafers about the size of a quarter. After they become hardened they may be dipped in chocolate. In fact, practically any of the fondant candies may be coated with chocolate in the following way:

Melt the commercial chocolate prepared for this purpose in a double boiler. Be careful not to let the water in the lower part boil, for this makes the chocolate coating streaked when it hardens. With a two-tined fork lower the fondant candies, fruit balls, or nuts into the melted chocolate. Lift them quickly and scrape off with a knife the surplus chocolate that drips from them. Place on waxed paper to dry.

Aunt Sammy's Radio Recipes, Records of the U.S. Department of Agriculture

President Truman smiles broadly as he cuts his cake on the celebration of his 61st birthday, 1945. *Harry S. Truman Presidential Library and Museum.*

ACKNOWLEDGMENTS

For many years, we have been interested in publishing a book of recipes from the rich holdings of the National Archives, including its 13 Presidential libraries and museums. We were delighted that the National Archives Experience's latest exhibition, "What's Cooking, Uncle Sam? The Government's Effect on the American Diet" gave us a perfect opportunity to move forward.

We are very grateful to Archivist of the United States David S. Ferriero—a chef and cookbook editor himself—for his interest in the project and his wonderful contribution to the book. We also thank our partners and friends at the National Archives Experience, especially Marvin Pinkert, director of the Center for the National Archives Experience, Christina Rudy Smith, Director of Exhibits, and Alice Kamps, Curator, who generously shared their research and expertise to make the recipe book possible.

The Foundation for the National Archives' Director of Publications Patty Reinert Mason managed the project and edited the recipe book, while Publications and Research Assistant Kathleen Lietzau researched the recipes and images.

Brian Barth of the National Archives deserves all credit and our thanks for the book's beautiful design, and we thank the Archives' Maureen MacDonald for her counsel and copyediting expertise.

A special thank you goes to Chef José Andrés, the exhibition's Chief Culinary Advisor and President of ThinkFoodGroup, who generously contributed the introduction for the recipe book and, along with his colleagues at ThinkFoodGroup, helped us to create an incredible partnership in support of the exhibition, including a delicious dining experience at America Eats near the National Archives Building in Washington, DC.

We also thank Ted Segal, a member of the Foundation's Board of Directors, the Foundation's Director of Development Stefanie Mathew, and Director of Administration and Marketing Franck Cordes, as well as the rest of the Foundation staff for their ongoing support.

We would also like to thank the following colleagues at the National Archives and Records Administration, including the 13 Presidential libraries and museums, who helped the Foundation secure recipes, images, and artwork for the recipe book: Karen Abramson, Laurie Austin, Rutha Beamon, Gale Bentley, Rick Blondo, Stacey Bredhoff, Bonnie Burlbaw, Barbara Cline, Vernon Early, Pamla Eisenberg, Michelle Farnsworth, Xaviera Flores, Karen Hibbitt, Alexis Hill, Tim Holtz, Michael Horsley, Spencer Howard, Mary Ilario, Martin Jacobson, John Keller, Tammy Kelly, Patrick Kepley, Jessica Kratz, Abigail Malangone, Jennifer Mandel, Ed McCarter, Darlene McClurkin, Mark Meader, Nancy Mirshah, McKenzie Morse, Nancy Mottershaw, Christine Mouw, Brittany Parris, Amanda Perez, Stephen Plotkin, Holly Reed, Jeffrey Reed, Richard Schneider, Jennifer Seitz, Lynn Smith, Jodie Steck, Kathy Struss, Alycia Vivona, Alison Wheelock, and James Zeender.

I would like to personally express my appreciation to all those who assisted us with this project!

Thora Colot
Executive Director
Foundation for the National Archives